College Marlborough

Hymns for Use in the Chapel of Marlborough College

College Marlborough

Hymns for Use in the Chapel of Marlborough College

ISBN/EAN: 9783744781879

Printed in Europe, USA, Canada, Australia, Japan

Cover: Foto ©Thomas Meinert / pixelio.de

More available books at **www.hansebooks.com**

HYMNS

FOR USE IN THE CHAPEL OF

MARLBOROUGH COLLEGE.

PRIVATELY PRINTED.

LONDON:

PRINTED BY RICHARD CLAY AND SONS,

BREAD STREET HILL.

1886.

PREFACE.

THE present edition differs from that of 1878 chiefly in the addition of an Appendix containing thirty-nine new Hymns and, as in the first edition, a number of Sacred Poems.

The Editors tender their best thanks to the many Authors and Publishers who have kindly allowed the use of copyright Hymns in this, or former editions; and specially to Messrs. Novello, Ewer and Co., for permission to print Nos. 3 and 12, in the Appendix; to the Proprietors of "Hymns Ancient and Modern" for Nos. 9 and 31; to Messrs. Nisbet and Co. for No. 20, and No. 12 of the Sacred Poems.

The Editors have been at pains to obtain permission for the use of all copyright Hymns; if any have been inserted without permission, they ask forgiveness for the inadvertence.

MARLBOROUGH.
August 1886.

ERRATA.

Page 194, *for* " For why ? " *read* " For-why."

    ,,   380, *for* " coelica," *read* " caelica."

    ,,   393, *for* " F. D. Maurice ✠ 1872," *read* " F. D. Morice."

    ,,   394, line 1, in some copies " O FOR " is misprinted.

    ,,   402, *for* " coelesti," *read* " caelesti."

HYMNS.

AWAKE, my soul, and with the sun
Thy daily stage of duty run;
Shake off dull sloth, and joyful rise
To pay thy morning sacrifice.

Thy precious time mis-spent redeem :
Each present day thy last esteem ;
Improve thy talent with due care ;
For the great day thyself prepare.

Wake and lift up thyself, my heart;
And with the angels bear thy part,
Who all night long unwearied sing
High praise to the Eternal King.

All praise to Thee, who safe hast kept,
And hast refreshed me whilst I slept !
Grant, Lord, when I from death shall wake,
I may of endless light partake !

Lord, I my vows to Thee renew ;
Disperse my sins as morning dew :
Guard my first springs of thought and will,
And with Thyself my spirit fill.

Direct, control, suggest, this day,
All I design, or do, or say ;
That all my powers, with all their might,
In Thy sole glory may unite.

Praise God, from Whom all blessings flow :
Praise Him, all creatures here below ;
Praise Him above, ye heavenly host ;
Praise Father, Son, and Holy Ghost.

Bishop Ken, 1700.

B

2

L. M.

NEW every morning is the love
Our wakening and uprising prove,
Through sleep and darkness safely brought,
Restored to life, and power, and thought.

New mercies, each returning day,
Hover around us while we pray ;
New perils past, new sins forgiven,
New thoughts of God, new hopes of heaven.

If, on our daily course, our mind
Be set to hallow all we find,
New treasures still, of countless price,
God will provide for sacrifice.

The trivial round, the common task,
Will furnish all we ought to ask ;
Room to deny ourselves ; a road
To bring us daily nearer God.

Only, O Lord, in Thy dear love
Fit us for perfect rest above ;
And help us, this and every day,
To live more nearly as we pray.

John Keble, 1827.

3

D. C. M.

YE that have spent the silent night
  In sleep and quiet rest,
And joy to see the cheerful light
  That riseth in the East ;
Now lift your hearts, your voices raise,
  Your morning tribute bring,
And pay a grateful song of praise
  To heaven's Almighty King.

And as this gloomy night did last
  But for a little space ;
As heavenly day, now night is past,
  Doth show his pleasant face :
So let us hope, when faith and love
  Their work on earth have done,
God's blessed face to see above,
  Heaven's better, brighter Sun.

God grant us grace that height to gain,
  That glorious sight to see,
And send us, after worldly pain,
  A life from trouble free ;
Where cheerful day shall ever shine,
  And sorrow never come :
Lord, be a place, a portion mine,
  In that bright blissful home.

George Gascoigne, ✠ 1577.

4

Six 7's.

CHRIST, whose glory fills the skies,
    Christ the true, the only Light,
Sun of Righteousness, arise,
    Triumph o'er the shades of night :
Day-spring from on high, be near ;
Day-star, in our hearts appear.

Dark and cheerless is the morn,
    Unaccompanied by Thee ;
Joyless is the day's return,
    Till Thy mercy's beams we see :
Till they pour their gladdening light
Through the darkness of our night.

Visit then these souls of Thine,
    Pierce the gloom of sin and grief,
Fill us, O Thou light divine,
    Scatter all our unbelief :
More and more Thyself display,
Shining to the perfect day.

Charles Wesley, 1740.

5

L. M.

LORD God of morning and of night,
We thank Thee for Thy gift of light ;
As in the dawn the shadows fly,
We seem to find Thee now more nigh.

Fresh hopes have wakened in the heart,
Fresh force to do our daily part ;
Thy thousand sleeps our strength restore
A thousandfold to serve Thee more.

Yet, whilst Thy will we would pursue,
Oft what we would we cannot do ;
The sun may stand in zenith skies,
But on the soul thick midnight lies.

O Lord of lights ! 'tis Thou alone
Canst make our darkened hearts Thine own :
Though this new day with joy we see,
Great dawn of God ! we cry for Thee !

Praise God, our Maker and our Friend ;
Praise Him through time, till time shall end ;
Till psalm and song His name adore
Through Heaven's great day of Evermore.

Francis T. Palgrave, 1862.

6

Six 7's.

AT Thy feet, O Christ, we lay
Thine own gift of this new day :
Doubt of what it holds in store
Makes us crave Thine aid the more :
Lest it prove a time of loss,
Mark it, Saviour, with Thy cross.

If it flow on calm and bright,
Be Thyself our chief delight ;
If it bring unknown distress,
Good is all that Thou canst bless :
Only, while its hours begin,
Pray we, keep them clear of sin.

We in part our weakness know,
And in part discern our foe ;
Well for us, before Thine eyes
All our danger open lies ;
Turn not from us, while we plead
Thy compassions and our need.

Fain would we Thy word embrace,
Live each moment in Thy grace,
All ourselves to Thee consign,
Fold up all our wills in Thine,
Think, and speak, and do, and be
Simply that which pleases Thee.

Hear us, Lord, and that right soon ;
Hear, and grant the choicest boon
That Thy love can e'er impart,
Loyal singleness of heart ;
So shall this and all our days,
Christ our GOD, show forth Thy praise.

William Bright, 1861.

7

L. M.

O JESU, Lord of heavenly grace,
Thou brightness of Thy Father's face,
Thou Fountain of eternal light,
Whose beams disperse the shades of night !

Come, holy Sun of heavenly love,
Shower down Thy radiance from above,
And to our inward hearts convey
The Holy Spirit's cloudless ray !

So we the Father's help will claim,
And sing the Father's glorious Name !
His powerful succour we implore,
That we may stand, to fall no more.

May He our actions deign to bless,
And loose the bonds of wickedness ;
From sudden falls our feet defend,
And bring us to a prosperous end !

O Christ ! with each returning morn
Thine image to our hearts is borne :
Oh, may we ever clearly see
Our Saviour and our God in Thee !

John Chandler, 1837,
from the Latin of St. Ambrose, ✠ 397,

8

D. 7. 6. 7. 6.

WHILE yet the morn is breaking
  I thank my God once more,
Beneath whose care awaking
  I find the night is o'er ;
I thank Him that He calls me
  To life and health anew,
I know, whate'er befalls me,
  His care will still be true.

Guardian of Israel, hear me,
  Watch o'er me through the day,
In all I do be near me :
  For others too I pray ;
To Thee I would commend them,
  Our church, our youth, our land,
Direct them and defend them
  When dangers are at hand.

O gently grant Thy blessing,
  That we may do Thy will,
No more Thy ways transgressing,
  Our proper task fulfil ;
Thy Spirit put within us,
  And let His gifts of grace
To all good actions win us,
  That best may show His praise.

Catherine Winkworth, 1862,
from the German of J. Mühlmann, 1618.

9

8. 7. 8. 7. 7. 7.

NOW the morn new light is pouring,
  Lord! may we our spirits raise,
Through Thy grace our souls restoring ;
  So, on Thy great day of days,
We with joy its dawn may meet
Fearless at Thy judgment-seat.

Jesus! Thou our steps be guiding
  By Thy Word's celestial light,
Now and evermore abiding
  Our defence, our rock of might!
Nowhere, save alone in Thee,
Can we rest from danger free.

Lo! we yield to Thy direction
  Soul and body, heart and mind ;
Keep Thou all by Thy protection,
  To Thy mighty hand resigned!
Thou our glorious God we own ;
Let us, Lord, be Thine alone!

Henry J. Buckoll, 1842,
from the German of Heinrich Albert, 1644.

10

7. 8. 7. 8. 7. 3.

COME, Thou bright and morning star,
Light of light, without beginning,
  Shine upon us from afar,
That we may be kept from sinning ;
  Drive away by Thy clear light
    Our dark night.

Let Thy grace, like morning dew
Falling upon barren places,
  Comfort, quicken, and renew
Our dry souls and dying graces :
  Bless Thy flock from Thy rich store
    Evermore.

May Thy fervent love destroy
Our cold works, in us awaking
  Ardent zeal, and holy joy.
At the purple morn's first breaking ;
  Let us truly rise, ere yet
    Life has set.

Ah ! Thou Day-star from on high,
Grant that at Thy next appearing,
  We who in the grave do lie,
May arise, Thy summons hearing ;
  And rejoice in our new life,
    Far from strife.

Light us to those heavenly spheres,
Sun of Grace, in glory shrouded ;
  Lead us through this vale of tears,
To the land where days unclouded,
  Purest joy, and perfect peace,
    Never cease.

Richard Massie. 1854,
from the German of C. K. von Rosenroth, 1684.

I I

n. 8. 4. 7.

COME, my soul, thou must be waking—
    Now is breaking
O'er the earth another day :
Come to Him Who made this splendour,
    See thou render
All thy feeble strength can pay.

Gladly hail the light returning ;
    Ready burning
Be the incense of thy powers :
For the night is safely ended—
    God hath tended
With His care thy helpless hours.

Pray that He may prosper ever
    Each endeavour,
When thine aim is good and true :
But that He may ever thwart thee,
    And convert thee,
When thou evil wouldst pursue.

Think that He thy ways beholdeth ;
    He unfoldeth
Every fault that lurks within ;
Every stain of shame glossed over
    Can discover
And discern each deed of sin.

Fettered to the fleeting hours,
    All our powers
Vain and brief are borne away :
Time, my soul, thy ship is steering,
    Onward veering,
To the gulf of death a prey.

Mayest thou then on life's last morrow,
    Free from sorrow,
Pass away in slumber sweet ;
And, released from death's dark sadness,
    Rise in gladness,
That far brighter Sun to greet.

                   Anon. 1838,
from the German of Baron von Canitz, ✠ 1699.

I 2

L. M.

FORTH in Thy name, O Lord, I go,
My daily labour to pursue,
Thee, only Thee, resolved to know
In all I think, or speak, or do.

The task Thy wisdom hath assigned
O let me cheerfully fulfil :
In all my works Thy presence find,
And prove Thy good and perfect will.

Thee may I set at my right hand,
Whose eyes mine inmost substance see,
And labour on at Thy command,
And offer all my works to Thee.

Give me to bear Thy easy yoke,
And every moment watch and pray ;
And still to things eternal look,
And hasten to Thy glorious day ;

For Thee delightfully employ
Whate'er Thy bounteous grace hath given,
And run my course with even joy,
And closely walk with Thee to heaven.

Charles Wesley, 1749.

13

L. M.

UP to the throne of God is borne
The voice of praise at early morn,
And He accepts the punctual hymn,
Sung as the light of day grows dim ;

Nor will He turn His ear aside
From holy offerings at noontide :
Then here to Him our souls we raise
In songs of gratitude and praise.

Blest are the moments, doubly blest,
That, drawn from this one hour of rest,
Are with a ready heart bestowed
Upon the service of our God.

Look up to heaven ! the industrious sun
Already half his race hath run ;
He cannot halt or go astray,
But our immortal spirits may.

Lord, since his rising in the east
If we have faltered or transgressed,
Guide, from Thy love's abundant source,
What yet remains of this day's course.

Help with Thy grace, through life's short day,
Our upward and our downward way ;
And glorify for us the west,
When we shall sink to final rest.

William Wordsworth, 1834.

14

L. M.

ALL praise to Thee, my God, this night,
For all the blessings of the light;
Keep me, O keep me, King of kings,
Beneath Thine own almighty wings.

Forgive me, Lord, for Thy dear Son,
The ill that I this day have done;
That with the world, myself, and Thee,
I, ere I sleep, at peace may be.

Teach me to live, that I may dread
The grave as little as my bed;
Teach me to die, that so I may
Rise glorious at the awful day.

O may my soul on Thee repose,
And may sweet sleep mine eyelids close,
Sleep that may me more vigorous make
To serve my God when I awake.

When in the night I sleepless lie,
My soul with heavenly thoughts supply;
Let no ill dreams disturb my rest,
No powers of darkness me molest.

Praise God, from Whom all blessings flow;
Praise Him, all creatures here below;
Praise Him above, ye heavenly host;
Praise Father, Son, and Holy Ghost.

Bishop Ken, 1700.

15

L. M.

SUN of my soul! Thou Saviour dear,
It is not night if Thou be near;
O may no earth-born cloud arise,
To hide Thee from Thy servant's eyes!

When the soft dews of kindly sleep
My wearied eyelids gently steep,
Be my last thought how sweet to rest
For ever on my Saviour's breast!

Abide with me from morn till eve,
For without Thee I cannot live:
Abide with me when night is nigh,
For without Thee I dare not die.

If some poor wandering child of Thine
Have spurned to-day the voice divine,
Now, Lord, the gracious work begin,
Let him no more lie down in sin.

Come near and bless us when we wake,
Ere through the world our way we take;
Till in the ocean of Thy love
We lose ourselves in heaven above.

John Keble, 1827.

16

C. M.

ALL praise to Him who dwells in bliss,
  Who made both day and night ;
Whose throne is darkness, in th' abyss
  Of uncreated light.

Each thought and deed His piercing eyes
  With strictest search survey ;
The deepest shades no more disguise
  Than the full blaze of day.

Whom Thou dost guard, O King of kings,
  No evil shall molest,
Under the shadow of Thy wings
  Shall they securely rest.

Thy angels shall around their beds
  Their constant stations keep :
Thy faith and truth shall shield their heads,
  For Thou dost never sleep.

Charles Wesley, 1741.

17

8. 7. 8. 7. 7. 7.

THROUGH the day Thy love hath spared us :
Now we lay us down to rest :
Through the silent watches guard us ;
Let no foe our peace molest :
Jesus, Thou our guardian be !
Sweet it is to trust in Thee.

Pilgrims here on earth, and strangers,
Dwelling in the midst of foes,
Us and ours preserve from dangers,
In Thine arms may we repose ;
And when life's sad day is past,
Rest with Thee in heaven at last !

Thomas Kelly, 1806.

18

Six 8's.

AS every day Thy mercy spares
Will bring its trials and its cares,
O Saviour, till my life shall end
Be Thou my Counsellor and Friend ;
Teach me Thy precepts all divine,
And be Thy great example mine.

When each day's scenes and labours close,
And wearied nature seeks repose,
With pardoning mercy richly blest,
Guard me, my Saviour, while I rest :
And as each morning sun shall rise,
Oh ! lead me onward to the skies.

And at my life's last setting sun,
My conflicts o'er, my labours done,
Jesu ! Thy heavenly radiance shed,
To cheer and bless my dying bed ;
Then from death's gloom my spirit raise
To see Thy face and sing Thy praise.

William Shrubsole, 1813.

19

8. 7. 8. 7.

SAVIOUR, breathe an evening blessing,
   Ere repose our spirits seal ;
Sin and want we come confessing,
   Thou canst save and Thou canst heal.

Though destruction walk around us,
   Though the arrows past us fly,
Angel-guards from Thee surround us,
   We are safe if Thou art nigh.

Though the night be dark and dreary,
   Darkness cannot hide from Thee ;
Thou art He, who, never weary,
   Watchest where Thy people be.

Should this night our spirit leave us,
   Should swift death our portion be,
Lord, in Paradise receive us,
   Rest we there in peace with Thee.

Varied from James Edmeston, 1820

♩ 20

(PSALM LXIII.) L. M.

O GOD, Thou art my God alone,
  Early to Thee my soul shall cry ;
A pilgrim in a land unknown,
  A thirsty land whose springs are dry.

Thee in the watches of the night
  When I remember on my bed,
Thy presence makes the darkness light ;
  Thy guardian wings are round my head.

Better than life itself Thy love,
  Dearer than all beside to me ;
For whom have I in heaven above,
  Or what on earth compared to Thee ?

Praise with my heart, my mind, my voice,
  For all Thy mercy I will give ;
My soul shall still in Thee rejoice ;
  My tongue shall bless Thee while I live.

James Montgomery, 1822.

21

Six 7's.

FATHER ! by Thy love and power
Comes again the evening hour ;
Light has vanished, labours cease,
Weary creatures rest in peace :
We to Thee ourselves resign ;
Let our latest thoughts be Thine.

Saviour ! to Thy Father bear
This our feeble evening prayer ;
Thou hast seen how oft to-day
We like sheep have gone astray :
Blessed Saviour, yet through Thee
Grant that we may pardoned be.

Holy Spirit ! breathing balm.
Fall on us in evening's calm ;
Yet a while before we sleep,
We with Thee will vigil keep :
Melt our spirits, mould our will,
Soften, strengthen, comfort still.

Blessed Trinity ! be near
Through the hours of darkness drear ;
Watch o'er our defenceless head,
Keep all evil from our bed ;
Till the flood of morning rays
Wake us to a song of praise.

Joseph Anstice, 1836

22

8. 6. 8. 6. 8.

LORD of my life, whose tender care
   Hath led me on till now,
Here lowly at the hour of prayer
   Before Thy throne I bow ;
I bless Thy gracious hand, and pray
Forgiveness for another day.

Oh may I daily, hourly strive
   In heavenly grace to grow ;
To Thee and to Thy glory live,
   Dead else to all below ;
Tread in the path my Saviour trod,
Though thorny, yet the path to God !

With prayer my humble praise I bring
   For mercies day by day :
Lord, teach my heart Thy love to sing,
   Lord, teach me how to pray !
All that I have, and am, to Thee
I offer through Eternity !

Anon. 1838.

23

L. M.

AGAIN, as evening's shadow falls,
We gather in these hallowed walls ;
And vesper hymn and vesper prayer
Rise mingling on the holy air.

May struggling hearts that seek release
Here find the rest of God's own peace ;
And, strengthened here by hymn and prayer,
Lay down the burden and the care !

O God our light ! to Thee we bow ;
Within all shadows standest Thou ;
Give deeper calm than night can bring ;
Give sweeter songs than lips can sing.

Life's tumult we must meet again,
We cannot at the shrine remain ;
But in the spirit's secret cell
May hymn and prayer for ever dwell.

Samuel Longfellow, 1846.

24

Four 10's.

ABIDE with me ! fast falls the eventide ;
The darkness deepens : Lord, with me abide :
When other helpers fail, and comforts flee,
Help of the helpless, O abide with me !

Swift to its close ebbs out life's little day ;
Earth's joys grow dim, its glories pass away ;
Change and decay in all around I see ;
O Thou who changest not, abide with me !

I need Thy presence every passing hour ;
What but Thy grace can foil the tempter's power ?
Who like Thyself my guide and stay can be ?
Through cloud and sunshine, O abide with me !

I fear no foe, with Thee at hand to bless ;
Ills have no weight, and tears no bitterness ;
Where is death's sting ? where, grave, thy victory ?
I triumph still, if Thou abide with me !

Hold then Thy Cross before my closing eyes ;
Shine through the gloom, and point me to the skies ;
Heaven's morning breaks, and earth's vain shadows
    flee ;
In life, in death, O Lord, abide with me !

Henry F. Lyte, 1847.

25

Six 8's.

SWEET Saviour, bless us ere we go ;
   Thy word into our minds instil ;
And make our lukewarm hearts to glow
   With lowly love and fervent will.
Through life's long day and death's dark night,
O gentle Jesus, be our Light.

The day is gone, its hours have run,
   And Thou hast taken count of all,
The scanty triumphs grace hath won,
   The broken vow, the frequent fall.
Through life's long day, &c.

Grant us, dear Lord, from evil ways
   True absolution and release ;
And bless us, more than in past days,
   With purity and inward peace.
Through life's long day, &c.

Do more than pardon, give us joy,
   Sweet fear, and sober liberty,
And simple hearts without alloy
   That only long to be like Thee.
Through life's long day, &c.

Labour is sweet, for Thou hast toiled !
   And care is light, for Thou hast cared ;
Ah ! never let our works be soiled
   With strife, or by deceit ensnared.
Through life's long day, &c.

For all we love, the poor, the sad,
   The sinful, unto Thee we call ;
O let Thy mercy make us glad :
   Thou art our Jesus, and our All.
Through life's long day, &c.

Frederick W. Faber, 1849.

26

L. M.

O FATHER, who didst all things make,
  That heaven and earth might do Thy will,
Bless us, this eve, for Jesus' sake,
  And for Thy work preserve us still.

O Son, who didst redeem mankind,
  And set the captive sinner free,
Keep us, this eve, with peaceful mind,
  That we may safe abide with Thee.

O Holy Ghost, who by Thy power
  The Church elect dost sanctify,
Seal us, this eve, and, hour by hour,
  These hearts and members purify.

William B. Heathcote, 1846.

27

7. 7. 7. 5.

HOLY Father, cheer our way
With Thy love's perpetual ray ;
Grant us every closing day
  Light at evening time.

Holy Saviour, calm our fears
When earth's brightness disappears ;
Grant us in our latter years
  Light at evening time.

Holy Spirit, be Thou nigh
When in mortal pains we lie ;
Grant us, as we come to die,
  Light at evening time.

Holy, Blessed Trinity !
Darkness is not dark with Thee ;
Those Thou keepest always see
  Light at evening time.

Richard H. Robinson, 1861.

28

Four 10's.

SAVIOUR, again to Thy dear Name we raise
With one accord our parting hymn of praise ;
We stand to bless Thee ere our worship cease ;
Then, lowly kneeling, wait Thy word of peace.

Grant us Thy peace upon our homeward way ;
With Thee began, with Thee shall end the day :
Guard Thou the lips from sin, the hearts from shame,
That in this house have called upon Thy name.

Grant us Thy peace, Lord, through the coming night;
Turn Thou for us its darkness into light:
From harm and danger keep Thy children free,
For dark and light are both alike to Thee.

Grant us Thy peace throughout our earthly life :
Peace to Thy Church from error and from strife ;
Peace to our land, the fruit of truth and love ;
Peace in each heart, Thy Spirit from above.

Thy peace in sorrow, balm of every pain ;
Thy peace in death, the hope to rise again ;
In that dread hour speak Thou the soul's release,
And call it, Lord, to Thine eternal peace.

John Ellerton, 1858.

29

P. M.

STAR of morn and even,
Sun of Heaven's heaven,
    Saviour high and dear,
    Toward us turn Thine ear ;
    Through whate'er may come,
    Thou canst lead us home.

Though the gloom be grievous,
Those we leant on leave us,
    Though the coward heart
    Quit its proper part,
    Though the tempter come,
    Thou wilt lead us home.

Saviour, pure and holy,
Lover of the lowly,
    Sign us with Thy sign,
    Take our hands in Thine ;
    Take our hands and come,
    Lead Thy children home !

Star of morn and even,
Shine on us from heaven ;
    From Thy glory-throne
    Hear Thy very own !
    Lord and Saviour, come,
    Lead us to our home !

Francis T. Palgrave, 1862.

30

L. M.

O LIGHT of life, O Saviour dear,
Before we sleep bow down Thine ear,
Through dark and day, o'er land and sea,
We have no other hope but Thee.

Oft from Thy royal road we part,
Lost in the mazes of the heart:
Our lamps put out, our course forgot,
We seek for God and find Him not.

What sudden sunbeams cheer our sight!
What dawning risen upon the night!
Thou giv'st Thyself to us, and we
Find Guide and Path and all in Thee.

Through day and darkness, Saviour dear,
Abide with us more nearly near;
Till on Thy face we lift our eyes,
The Sun of God's own Paradise.

Praise God our Maker and our Friend;
Praise Him through time, till time shall end;
Till psalm and song His name adore
Through Heaven's great day of Evermore.

Francis T. Palgrave, 1862.

31

8. 8. 8. 4.

THE radiant morn hath passed away,
And spent too soon her golden store ;
The shadows of departing day
    Creep on once more.

Our life is but a fading dawn,
Its glorious noon how quickly past ;
Lead us, O Christ, when all is gone,
    Safe home at last.

Oh, by Thy soul-inspiring grace
Uplift our hearts to realms on high ;
Help us to look to that bright place
    Beyond the sky ;

Where light, and love, and joy, and peace
In undivided empire reign,
And thronging angels never cease
    Their deathless strain ;

Where saints are clothed in spotless white,
And evening shadows never fall,
Where Thou, Eternal Light of light,
    Art Lord of all !

Godfrey Thring, 1866.

32

L. M.

AT even, ere the sun was set,
The sick, O Lord, around Thee lay ;
Oh, in what divers pains they met !
Oh, with what joy they went away !

Once more 'tis eventide, and we,
Oppressed with various ills, draw near ;
What if Thy form we cannot see ?
We know and feel that Thou art here.

O Saviour Christ, our woes dispel ;
For some are sick, and some are sad,
And some have never loved Thee well,
And some have lost the love they had ;

And some have found the world is vain,
Yet from the world they break not free ;
And some have friends who give them pain,
Yet have not sought a friend in Thee ;

And none, O Lord, have perfect rest,
For none are wholly free from sin ;
And they, who fain would serve Thee best,
Are conscious most of wrong within.

O Saviour Christ, Thou too art man ;
Thou hast been troubled, tempted, tried ;
Thy kind but searching glance can scan
The very wounds that shame would hide ;

Thy touch has still its ancient power ;
No word from Thee can fruitless fall ;
Hear, in this solemn evening hour,
And in Thy mercy heal us all.

Henry Twells, 1861.

33

L. M.

NOW at the night's return we raise
To Thee, our King, the voice of praise;
And may our prayer, set forth aright,
Ascend like incense in Thy sight.

Full well we know in whom we trust,
Whose hand exalts us from the dust,
Whose will assigns each day and hour,
Whose grace in weakness perfects power.

O'er all that stains our life-time past
The veil of Thy forgiveness cast;
Yea, cleanse our spirits through and through,
And set us right, and keep us true.

Bless Thou the distant and the dear,
Let each to each in Thee draw near,
Still travelling towards our home above
And leaning still on one strong love.

To Thee, O Christ, we lift our eyes,
On Thee alone our hope relies;
Thou wilt not, canst not, bring to shame
The hope that pleads Thy glorious name.

William Bright, 1874.

34

8. 4. 8. 4. 8. 8. 8. 4.

GOD, that madest earth and heaven,
 Darkness and light,
Who the day for toil hast given,
 For rest the night ;
May Thine angel-guards defend us,
Slumber sweet Thy mercy send us,
Holy dreams and hopes attend us,
 This livelong night !

Guard us waking, guard us sleeping,
 And, when we die,
May we in Thy mighty keeping
 All peaceful lie :
When the last dread call shall wake us,
Do not Thou, our Lord, forsake us,
But to reign in glory take us
 With Thee on high !

First Stanza by Bishop Heber, 1827.
Second Stanza from the Latin by
 Archbishop Whately, 1863.

35

L. M.

BEFORE the ending of the day,
Creator of the world ! we pray
That with Thy wonted favour Thou
Wouldst be our Guard and Keeper now.

Uplift us with Thine arm of might,
So may our souls rise pure and bright ;
With love divine our hearts inflame,
To praise Thee for Thy glorious Name.

Within our spirits ever dwell,
And worldly darkness thence expel ;
The faith of old by saints professed
Root deep within our inmost breast.

Author of all things, gracious Guide,
In life be ever at our side ;
And when the assaults of death impend,
Thy people strengthen and defend.

John M. Neale, 1851,
from the Latin of St. Ambrose, ✠ 397.

36

6. 4. 6. 6.

THE sun is sinking fast,
   The daylight dies ;
Let love awake, and pay
   Her evening sacrifice.

As Christ upon the Cross
   His Head inclined,
And to His Father's hands
   His parting soul resigned ;

So now herself my soul
   Would wholly give
Into His sacred charge,
   In Whom all spirits live ;

So now beneath His eye
   Would calmly rest,
Without a wish or thought
   Abiding in the breast ;

Save that His will be done,
   Whate'er betide ;
Dead to herself, and dead
   In Him to all beside.

Thus would I live ; yet now
   Not I, but He
In all His power and love
   Henceforth alive in me.

One sacred Trinity :
   One Lord divine :
May I be ever His,
   And He for ever mine !

Edward Caswall, 1858,
from a Latin hymn of the eighteenth century.

37

7. 6. 7. 6. 8. 8.

THE day is past and over;
　All thanks, O Lord, to Thee.
We pray Thee now that sinless
　The hours of darkness be.
O Jesu! keep us in Thy sight,
And guard us through the coming night.

The joys of day are over;
　We lift our hearts to Thee,
And ask that pure and holy
　The hours of darkness be.
O Jesu! make their darkness light,
And guard us through the coming night.

The toils of day are over;
　We raise our hymn to Thee,
And ask that free from peril
　The hours of darkness be.
O Jesu! keep us in Thy sight,
And guard us through the coming night.

John M. Neale, 1862,
from the Greek of St. Anatolius, ✠ 458.

38

L. M.

THE happy sunshine all is gone,
The gloomy night comes swiftly on ;
But shine Thou still, O Christ our Light,
Nor let us lose ourselves in night.

We thank Thee, Father, that this day
Thy angels watched around our way,
And free from harm and vexing fear
Have led us on in safety here.

Lord, have we angered Thee to-day,
Remember not our sins, we pray,
But let Thy mercy o'er them sweep,
And give us calm and restful sleep.

Thine angels guard our sleeping hours,
And keep afar all evil powers ;
And Thou all pain and mischief ward
From soul and body, faithful Lord !

Catherine Winkworth, 1855,
from the German of N. Hermann, 1560.

39

10. 10. 10 4.

THE night is come, wherein at last we rest ;
God order this and all things for the best !
Beneath His blessing fearless we may lie,
    Since He is nigh.

Drive evil thoughts and spirits far away,
O Master, watch o'er us till dawning day,
Body and soul alike from harm defend,
    Thine angel send.

Let holy prayers and thoughts our latest be,
Let us awake with joy, still close to Thee,
In all serve Thee, in every deed and thought
    Thy praise be sought.

Give to the sick, as Thy beloved, sleep,
And help the captive, comfort those who weep,
Care for the widows' and the orphans' woe,
    Keep far our foe.

For we have none on whom for help to call,
Save Thee, O God in heaven, who car'st for all,
And wilt forsake them never day or night,
    Who love Thee right.

Father, Thy Name be praised, Thy kingdom come,
Thy will be wrought as in our heavenly home,
Keep us in life, forgive our sins, deliver
    Us now and ever.

Catherine Winkworth, 1858, from Michael Weiss'
German translation, 1531, from the Bohemian
Brethren, 1504.

40

7. 7. 6. 7. 7. 8.

NOW all the woods are sleeping,
And night and stillness creeping
 O'er earth with toil opprest :
But thou my heart awake thee,
To prayer a while betake thee,
 And praise thy Maker ere thou rest.

Now thought and labour ceases,
For night the tired releases,
 And bids sweet rest begin ;
My heart, there comes a morrow
Shall set thee free from sorrow
 And all the dreary toil of sin.

My Saviour, stay Thou by me,
And let no foe come nigh me,
 Safe sheltered by Thy wing ;
But would the foe alarm me,
Oh, let him never harm me,
 But still Thine angels round me sing !

Catherine Winkworth, 1862,
from the German of Paul Gerhardt, 1653.

41

(Psalm XCII.)   L. M.

SWEET is the work, my God, my King,
To praise Thy Name, give thanks and sing,
To show Thy love by morning light,
And talk of all Thy truth at night!

Sweet is the day of sacred rest;
No mortal cares shall seize my breast;
O may my heart in tune be found,
Like David's harp of solemn sound!

My heart shall triumph in my Lord,
And bless His works, and bless His Word;
Thy works of grace, how bright they shine!
How deep Thy counsels, how divine!   .

Soon shall I see and hear and know
All I desired or wished below,
And every power find sweet employ
In that eternal world of joy.

                        Isaac Watts, 1719.

42

6. 6. 6. 6. 8. 8.

COME, sons of God, awake,
To hail this sacred day,
And in glad songs of praise
Your grateful homage pay ;
Come, bless the day that God hath blest,
The type of Heaven's eternal rest.

Upon this happy morn,
The Lord of Life arose ;
He burst the bands of death,
And vanquished all our foes ;
And now He pleads our cause above,
And reaps the fruit of all His love.

Then hail, triumphant Lord !
Heaven with Hosannas rings,
And earth, with humbler strains,
Thy praise in answer sings :
Worthy the Lamb, that once was slain,
Through endless years to live and reign !

Thomas Cotterill, 1812.

43

S. M.

THIS is the day of light :
Let there be light to-day ;
O Day-spring, rise upon our night,
And chase its gloom away.

This is the day of rest :
Our failing strength renew ;
On weary brain and troubled breast
Shed Thou Thy freshening dew.

This is the day of peace :
Thy peace our spirits fill ;
Bid Thou the blasts of discord cease,
The waves of strife be still.

This is the day of prayer :
Let earth to heaven draw near ;
Lift up our hearts to seek Thee there,
Come down to meet us here.

This is the first of days :
Send forth Thy quickening breath,
And wake dead souls to love and praise,
O Vanquisher of death.

John Ellerton, 1861.

44

P. M.

AS Thou didst rest, O Father, o'er nature's finished
    birth,
As Thou didst in Thy work rejoice, and bless the
    new-born earth,
So give us now that Sabbath-rest, which makes
    Thy children free,
Free for the work of love to man, of thankfulness
    to Thee.

But in Thy worship, Father, oh, lift our souls above,
By holy word, by prayer and hymn, by eucharistic
    love ;
Till e'en the dull cold work of earth, the earth
    which Christ hath trod,
Shall be itself a silent prayer, to raise us up to
    God.

So lead us on to heaven, where, in Thy presence
    blest,
The wicked cease from troubling, and the weary
    are at rest,
Where faith is lost in vision, where love hath no
    alloy,
And through eternity there flows the deepening
    stream of joy.

To Thee, who giv'st us freedom, our Father and
    our King ;
To Thee, the risen Lord of Life, our ransomed
    spirits sing ;
Thou fill'st the Church in earth and heaven, O
    Holy Ghost ; to Thee
In warfare's toil, in victory's rest, eternal glory be.
                  Alfred Barry.

45

Four 7's.

MORN of morns, and day of days !
Beauteous were thy new-born rays :
Brighter yet from death's dark prison
Christ, the Light of lights, is risen.

He commanded, and His word
Death and the dread chaos heard ;
Oh, shall we, more deaf than they,
In the chains of darkness stay ?

Unto hearts in slumber weak
Let the heavenly trumpet speak ;
And a newer walk express
Their new life to righteousness.

Grant us this, and with us be,
O Thou Fount of charity,
Thou who dost the Spirit give,
Bidding the dead letter live.

Glory to the Father, Son,
And to Thee, O Holy One,
By whose quickening breath divine
Our dull spirits burn and shine.

Isaac Williams, 1843,
from the Latin of Charles Coffin, 1755.
(Varied by Sir Henry W. Baker, 1861.)

46

7. 8. 7. 8. 8. 8.

BLESSED Jesus, at Thy word
We are gathered all to hear Thee ;
Let our hearts and souls be stirred
Now to seek and love and fear Thee ;
By Thy teachings sweet and holy
Drawn from earth to love Thee solely.

All our knowledge, sense, and sight,
Lie in deepest darkness shrouded,
Till Thy Spirit breaks our night
With the beams of truth unclouded ;
Thou alone to God canst win us,
Thou must work all good within us.

Glorious Lord, Thyself impart !
Light of light from God proceeding,
Open Thou our ears and heart,
Help us by Thy Spirit's pleading ;
Hear the cry Thy people raises,
Hear, and bless our prayers and praises.

Catherine Winkworth, 1858,
from the German of T. Clausnitzer, 1671.

47

7. 8. 7. 8. 8. 8.

LIGHT of light, enlighten me,
Now anew the day is dawning;
　Sun of grace, the shadows flee,
Brighten Thou my Sabbath morning;
With Thy joyous sunshine blest
Happy is my day of rest.

Fount of all our joy and peace,
To Thy living waters lead me,
　Thou from earth my soul release,
And with grace and mercy feed me;
Bless Thy word that it may prove
Rich in fruits that Thou dost love.

Kindle Thou the sacrifice
That upon my lips is lying;
　Clear the shadows from mine eyes
That, from every error flying,
No strange fire within me glow
That Thine altar doth not know.

Let me with my heart to-day,
Holy, Holy, Holy, singing,
　Rapt a while from earth away,
All my soul to Thee upspringing,
Have a foretaste inly given
How they worship Thee in heaven.

Catherine Winkworth, 1858,
from the German of Benjamin Schmolck, 1731.

48

Four 7's.

ERE another Sabbath's close,
Ere again we seek repose,
Lord, our song ascends to Thee,
At Thy feet we bow the knee.

For the mercies of the day,
For this rest upon our way,
Thanks to Thee alone be given,
Lord of earth and King of heaven.

Cold our services have been,
Mingled every prayer with sin ;
But Thou canst and wilt forgive ;
By Thy grace alone we live.

Whilst this thorny path we tread,
May Thy love our footsteps lead ;
When our journey here is past,
May we rest with Thee at last.

Let these earthly Sabbaths prove
Foretastes of our joys above ;
While their steps Thy pilgrims bend
To the rest which knows no end.

Anon. 1832.

49

Eight 8's.

THE Lord is come! On Syrian soil
The child of poverty and toil—
The Man of Sorrows, born to know
Each varying shade of human woe :
His joy, His glory to fulfil
In earth and heaven His Father's will :
On lonely mount, by festive board,
On bitter cross, despised, adored.

The Lord is come ! Dull hearts to wake,
He speaks, as never man yet spake,
The truth which makes His servants free,
The royal law of liberty ;
Though heaven and earth shall pass away
His living words our spirits stay,
And from His treasures, new and old,
The eternal mysteries unfold.

The Lord is come ! With joy behold
The gracious signs, declared of old ;
The ear that hears, the eye that sees,
The sick restored to health and ease ;
The poor, that from their low estate
Are roused to seek a nobler fate ;
The minds with doubt and dread possest,
That find in Him their perfect rest.

The Lord is come ! In every heart,
Where truth and mercy claim a part ;
In every land, where right is might
And deeds of darkness shun the light ;
In every church, where faith and love
Lift earthward thoughts to things above ;
In every holy, happy home,
We bless Thee, Lord, that Thou art come.

Arthur P. Stanley, ✠ 1881.

E

50

Six 7's.

DAY of wrath, O dreadful day,
When this world shall pass away,
And the heavens together roll,
Shrivelling like a parchèd scroll—
Long foretold by saint and sage,
David's harp, and Sibyl's page.

Day of terror, day of doom,
When the Judge at last shall come ;
Through the deep and silent gloom,
Shrouding every human tomb,
Shall the Archangel's trumpet-tone
Summon all before the Throne.

Then shall nature stand aghast,
Death himself be overcast ;
Then, at her Creator's call,
Near and distant, great and small,
Shall the whole creation rise,
Waiting for the great assize.

Then the writing shall be read,
Which shall judge the quick and dead :
Then the Lord of all our race
Shall appoint to each his place ;
Every wrong shall be set right,
Every secret brought to light.

Then, in that tremendous day
When heaven and earth shall pass away,
What shall I, the sinner, say ?
What shall be the sinner's stay ?
When the righteous shrinks for fear,
How shall my frail soul appear ?

King of kings, enthroned on high
In Thine awful majesty,
Thou who of Thy mercy free
Savest those who saved shall be,
In Thy boundless charity,
Fount of Pity, save Thou me !

O remember, Saviour dear,
What the cause that brought Thee here :
All Thy long and perilous way
Was for me who went astray :
When that day at last is come,
Call, O call the wanderer home !

Thou in search of me didst sit
Weary with the noon-day heat,
Thou to save my soul hast borne
Cross, and grief, and hate, and scorn :
O, may all that toil and pain
Not be wholly spent in vain !

Righteous Judge, to Whom belongs
Vengeance for all earthly wrongs,
Grant forgiveness, Lord, at last,
Ere the dread account be past :
Lo ! my sighs, my guilt, my shame !
Spare me, for Thine own great name !

Thou who bad'st the sinner cease
From her tears, and go in peace ;
Thou who to the dying thief
Spakest pardon and relief ;
Thou, O Lord, to me hast given,
E'en to me, the hope of heaven !

Arthur P. Stanley, ✠ 1881.
from the "Dies irae" of Thomas of Celano, ✠ 1253.

51

L. M

THAT day of wrath, that dreadful day,
When heaven and earth shall pass away,
What power shall be the sinner's stay?
How shall he meet that dreadful day?

When, shrivelling like a parchèd scroll,
The flaming heavens together roll;
When louder yet, and yet more dread,
Swells the high trump that wakes the dead;

O! on that day, that wrathful day,
When man to judgment wakes from clay,
Be Thou, O Christ, the sinner's stay,
Though heaven and earth shall pass away.

Sir Walter Scott, 1805,
from the "Dies iræ" of Thomas of Celano, ✠ 1253.

52

8. 7. 8. 7. + 7.

LO ! He comes with clouds descending,
    Once for favoured sinners slain ;
Thousand thousand saints attending
    Swell the triumph of His train :
        Hallelujah !
    God appears on earth to reign.

Every eye shall now behold Him
    Robed in dreadful majesty ;
Those who set at nought and sold Him,
    Pierced and nailed Him to the tree,
        Deeply wailing,
    Shall the true Messiah see.

Now Redemption, long expected,
    See in solemn pomp appear !
All His saints, by man rejected,
    Now shall meet Him in the air.
        Hallelujah !
    See the day of God appear !

Yea, Amen ! let all adore Thee,
    High on Thine eternal throne ;
Saviour, take the power and glory,
    Claim the kingdoms for Thine own.
        O come quickly !
    Thou shalt reign, and Thou alone !

Varied from John Cennick, 1752,
    by Charles Wesley, 1758.

53

6. 6. 6. 6. 8. 8.

BLOW ye the trumpet, blow,
 The gladly solemn sound ;
Let all the nations know,
 To earth's remotest bound :
The year of Jubilee is come ;
Return, ye ransomed sinners, home.

Jesus, our great High Priest,
 Hath full atonement made ;
Ye weary spirits, rest ;
 Ye mournful souls, be glad :
The year of Jubilee is come ;
Return, ye ransomed sinners, home.

Extol the Lamb of God,
 The all-atoning Lamb ;
Redemption in His blood
 Throughout the world proclaim :
The year of Jubilee is come ;
Return, ye ransomed sinners, home.

Ye slaves of sin and hell,
 Your liberty receive ;
And safe in Jesus dwell,
 And blest in Jesus live :
The year of Jubilee is come ;
Return, ye ransomed sinners, home.

The Gospel trumpet hear,
 The news of heavenly grace ;
And, saved from earth, appear
 Before your Saviour's face :
The year of Jubilee is come ;
Return, ye ransomed sinners, home.

Charles Wesley, 1755.

54

8. 7. 8. 7.

COME, O Saviour long expected,
  Born to set Thy people free ;
From our guilt and fear protected,
  We shall find our rest in Thee.

Israel's strength and consolation,
  Hope of all the saints Thou art :
Blest desire of every nation,
  Joy of every Christian heart.

Born the chains of sin to sever,
  Born a child, and yet a king ;
Born to reign in us for ever,
  Now Thy gracious kingdom bring !

By Thine own eternal Spirit
  In our hearts rule Thou alone ;
By Thine all-sufficient merit
  Raise us to Thy glorious throne

  Varied from Charles Wesley, 1743.

55

THOU Judge of quick and dead,
  Before whose bar severe,
With holy joy, or guilty dread,
  We all must soon appear ;

Our anxious souls prepare
  For that tremendous day ;
And fill us now with watchful care,
  And stir us up to pray ;

To pray and wait the hour,
  The awful hour unknown,
When, robed in majesty and power,
  Thou shalt from heaven come down.

O may we all be found
  Obedient to Thy word,
Attentive to the trumpet's sound,
  And looking for our Lord.

O may we thus ensure
  Our lot among the blest,
And watch a moment, to secure
  An everlasting rest !

Charles Wesley, 1749.

56

C. M

HARK the glad sound ! the Saviour comes,
  The Saviour promised long !
Let every heart prepare a throne,
  And every voice a song.

He comes the prisoners to release
  In Satan's bondage held ;
The gates of brass before Him burst,
  The iron fetters yield.

He comes from thickest films of vice
  To clear the mental ray,
And on the eyelids of the blind
  To pour celestial day.

He comes to bind the broken heart,
  To make the wounded whole,
To preach glad tidings to the meek,
  And bless the humble soul.

Our glad hosannas, Prince of Peace !
  Thine advent shall proclaim ;
And earth and heaven shall join to sing
  The glories of Thy Name.

Philip Doddridge, 1735.

57

(PSALM LXXII.)　　　　L. M.

JESUS shall reign where'er the sun
Does his successive journeys run ;
His kingdom stretch from shore to shore,
Till moons shall wax and wane no more.

For Him shall endless prayer be made,
And praises throng to crown His Head ;
His Name, like sweet perfume, shall rise
With every morning sacrifice.

People and realms of every tongue
Dwell on His love with sweetest song,
And infant voices shall proclaim
Their early blessings on His Name.

Blessings abound where'er He reigns ;
The prisoner leaps to lose his chains ;
The weary find eternal rest,
And all the sons of want are blest.

Let every creature rise and bring
Peculiar honours to our King ;
Angels descend with songs again,
And earth repeat the loud Amen.

Isaac Watts, 1719.

58

(PSALM LXXII.) D. 7. 6. 7. 6.

HAIL to the Lord's Anointed,
  Great David's greater Son !
Hail in the time appointed,
  His reign on earth begun !
He comes to break oppression,
  To set the captive free,
To take away transgression,
  And rule in equity.

Kings shall fall down before Him,
  And gold and incense bring ;
All nations shall adore Him,
  His praise all people sing ;
For Him shall prayer unceasing,
  And daily vows ascend,
His kingdom still increasing,
  A kingdom without end.

O'er every foe victorious,
  He on His throne shall rest,
From age to age more glorious,
  All blessing and all-blest.
The tide of time shall never
  His covenant remove :
His Name shall stand for ever,
  That Name to us is Love.

James Montgomery, 1822.

59

L. M.

O SAVIOUR, is Thy promise fled,
  Nor longer might Thy grace endure
To heal the sick, and raise the dead,
  And preach Thy Gospel to the poor?

Come, Jesus, come! return again;
  With brighter beam Thy servants bless,
Who long to feel Thy perfect reign,
  And share Thy kingdom's happiness.

Come, Jesus, come! and, as of yore
  The prophet went to clear Thy way,
A harbinger Thy feet before,
  A dawning to Thy brighter day;

So now may grace with heavenly shower
  Our stony hearts for truth prepare;
Sow in our souls the seed of power,
  Then come and reap Thy harvest there.

Bishop Heber, 1827.

60

8. 7. 8. 7. 8. 8. 7.

THE Lord of might from Sinai's brow
  Gave forth His voice of thunder ;
And Israel lay on earth below,
  Outstretched in fear and wonder.
Beneath His feet was pitchy night,
And at His left hand and His right
  The rocks were rent asunder !

The Lord of love, on Calvary,
  A meek and suffering stranger,
Upraised to heaven His languid eye,
  In nature's hour of danger :
For us He bore the weight of woe,
For us He gave His blood to flow,
  And met His Father's anger.

The Lord of love, the Lord of might,
  The King of all created,
Shall back return to claim His right,
  On clouds of glory seated ;
With trumpet-sound and angel-song,
And hallelujahs loud and long,
  O'er death and hell defeated !

Bishop Heber, 1827.

61

8. 7. 8. 7.

HARK ! a thrilling voice is sounding ;
   " Christ is nigh," it seems to say ;
" Cast away the dreams of darkness,
   O ye children of the day !"

Wakened by the solemn warning,
   Let the earth-bound soul arise ;
Christ, her sun, all ill dispelling,
   Shines upon the morning skies.

Lo ! the Lamb, so long expected,
   Comes with pardon down from heaven :
Let us haste, with tears of sorrow,
   One and all to be forgiven ;

That, when next He comes with glory,
   And the world is wrapped in fear,
With His mercy He may shield us,
   And with words of love draw near.

Honour, glory, might, and blessing,
   To the Father and the Son,
With the everlasting Spirit,
   While eternal ages run.

Edward Caswall, 1849,

from an Ambrosian Hymn, fourth century,
(varied by compilers of Hymns A. and M., 1861.)

62

L. M.

ON Jordan's bank the Baptist's cry
Announces that the Lord is nigh ;
Awake, and hearken, for he brings
Glad tidings of the King of kings.

Then cleansed be every breast from sin ;
Make straight the way of God within ;
Prepare we in our hearts a home,
Where such a mighty Guest may come.

For Thou art our salvation, Lord,
Our refuge, and our great reward ;
Without Thy grace we waste away,
Like flowers that wither and decay.

To heal the sick stretch out Thine hand,
And bid the fallen sinner stand ;
Shine forth, and let Thy light restore
Earth's own true loveliness once more.

All praise, eternal Son, to Thee
Whose Advent doth Thy people free,
Whom with the Father we adore
And Holy Ghost for evermore.

John Chandler, 1837,
from the Latin of Charles Coffin, 1755,
(varied by compilers of Hymns A. and M., 1861.)

63

D. S. M.

A FEW more years shall roll,
A few more seasons come ;
And we shall be with those that rest
Asleep within the tomb.
Then, gracious Lord, prepare
Our souls for that dread day ;
O ! wash us in Thy precious blood,
And take our sins away.

A few more struggles here,
A few more partings o'er,
A few more toils, a few more tears,
And we shall weep no more.
Then, gracious Lord, prepare
Our souls for that bright day ;
O ! wash us in Thy precious blood,
And take our sins away.

A few more Sabbaths here
Shall cheer us on our way ;
And we shall reach the endless rest,
The eternal Sabbath-day.
Then, gracious Lord, prepare
Our souls for that sweet day ;
O ! wash us in Thy precious blood,
And take our sins away.

Yet but a little while,
And He shall come again,
Who died that we might live, who lives
That we with Him may reign.
Then, gracious Lord, prepare
Our souls for that glad day ;
O ! wash us in Thy precious blood,
And take our sins away.

Horatius Bonar, 1857.

64

L. M.

WHEN Christ from heaven came down of old
   He took our nature poor and low ;
He wore no form of angel mould,
   But shared our weakness and our woe.

But when He cometh back once more,
   Then shall be set the great white throne ;
And earth and heaven shall flee before
   The face of Him who sits thereon.

O Son of God ! in glory crowned,
   The Judge ordained of quick and dead ;
O Son of Man ! so pitying found
   For all the tears Thy people shed ;

Be with us in that awful hour,
   And by Thy crown, and by Thy grave,
By all Thy love and all Thy power,
   In that great day of Judgment save !

Cecil F. Alexander, 1858.

F

65

8. 7. 8. 7. 8. 8. 7.

GREAT God ! what do I see and hear ?
  The end of things created !
The Judge of mankind doth appear,
  On clouds of glory seated !
The trumpet sounds, the graves restore
The dead, which they contained before !
  Prepare, my soul, to meet Him !

The dead in Christ shall first arise,
  At the last trumpet's sounding,
Caught up to meet Him in the skies,
  With joy their Lord surrounding.
No gloomy fears their souls dismay,
His presence sheds eternal day
  On those prepared to meet Him.

But sinners filled with guilty fears,
  Behold his wrath prevailing ;
For they shall rise, and find their tears
  And sighs are unavailing :
The day of grace is past and gone ;
Trembling they stand before the throne,
  All unprepared to meet Him.

O Jesu ! friend to fallen man,
  To me impart Thy merit ;
Forgive my sin, wash out its stain,
  By Thine Almighty Spirit !
The trumpet sounds ; the Judge is near ;
But then my soul, devoid of fear,
  Shall spring with joy to meet Him.

*First stanza anonymous from the German
of Bartholomew Ringwaldt,* 1585 ; *the
rest by William B. Collyer,* 1812.

66

(PSALM XXIV.)

8. 8. 8. 8. 8 8. 6. 8.

LIFT up your heads, ye mighty gates,
Behold the King of Glory waits,
The King of kings is drawing near,
The Saviour of the world is here ;
Life and salvation doth He bring,
Wherefore rejoice, and gladly sing
    Praise, O my God, to Thee !
    Creator, wise is Thy decree !

The Lord is just, a helper tried,
Mercy is ever at His side,
His kingly crown is holiness,
His sceptre pity in distress,
The end of all our woe He brings ;
Wherefore the earth is glad and sings
    Praise, O my God, to Thee !
    O Saviour, great Thy deeds shall be !

Oh, blest the land, the city blest,
Where Christ the ruler is confest !
Oh, happy hearts and happy homes
To whom this King in triumph comes !
The cloudless sun of joy He is,
Who bringeth pure delight and bliss ;
    Praise, O my God, to Thee !
    Comforter, for Thy comfort free !

Fling wide the portals of your heart,
Make it a temple set apart
From earthly use for heaven's employ,
Adorned with prayer, and love, and joy :
So shall your Sovereign enter in,
And new and nobler life begin.
    Praise, O my God, be Thine,
    For word, and deed, and grace divine !
      Catherine Winkworth, 1855,
  from the German of George Weiszel, 1635.

67

L. M.

WHILE shepherds watched their flocks by night,
  All seated on the ground,
The angel of the Lord came down,
  And glory shone around.

" Fear not," said he ; for mighty dread
  Had seized their troubled mind ;
" Glad tidings of great joy I bring
  To you and all mankind.

"To you in David's town this day
  Is born of David's line
A Saviour, who is Christ the Lord ;
  And this shall be the sign :

" The heavenly Babe you there shall find
  To human view displayed,
All meanly wrapped in swathing bands,
  And in a manger laid."

Thus spake the seraph ; and forthwith
  Appeared a shining throng
Of angels praising God, who thus
  Addressed their joyful song :

"All glory be to God on high,
  And on the earth be peace ;
Good-will henceforth from heaven to men
  Begin and never cease."

Tate and Brady, 1703.

68

P. M.

ANGELS, from the realms of glory,
  Wing your flight o'er all the earth ;
Ye who sang Creation's story,
  Now proclaim Messiah's birth :
    Come and worship,
Worship Christ the new-born King !

Shepherds, in the field abiding,
  Watching o'er your flocks by night,
God with man is now residing,
  Round you shines the heavenly light ;
    Come and worship,
Worship Christ the new-born King !

Saints, before the altar bending,
  Watching long in hope and fear,
Suddenly the Lord descending
  In His temple shall appear ;
    Come and worship,
Worship Christ the new-born King.

James Montgomery, 1819.

69

Irregular.

O COME, all ye faithful,
Joyful and triumphant,
O come ye, O come ye, to Bethlehem ;
Come and behold Him,
Born the King of angels ;
O come, let us adore Him,
O come, let us adore Him,
O come, let us adore Him, Christ the Lord.

God of God,
Light of Light,
Lo, He abhors not the Virgin's womb ;
Very God,
Begotten not created ;
O come, let us adore Him, &c.

Sing, choirs of angels,
Sing in exultation,
Sing, all ye citizens of heaven above,
· Glory to God
In the highest ;
O come, let us adore Him, &c.

Yea, Lord, we greet Thee,
Born this happy morning :
Jesus, to Thee be glory given ;
Word of the Father,
Now in flesh appearing :
O come, let us adore Him,
O come, let us adore Him,
O come, let us adore Him, Christ the Lord.

Frederick Oakley, 1841,
from a Latin Hymn of fifteenth century.
(*Varied by compilers of Hymns A. and M.*, 1861.)

70

Ten 7's.

HARK! the herald angels sing
Glory to the new-born King,
Peace on earth and mercy mild,
God and sinners reconciled!
Joyful, all ye nations, rise,
Join the triumph of the skies;
With the Angelic host proclaim,
Christ is born in Bethlehem.
  Hark! the herald angels sing
  Glory to the new-born King.

Christ by highest heaven adored;
Christ the Everlasting Lord;
Late in time behold Him come,
Offspring of a Virgin's womb;
Veiled in flesh the Godhead see;
Hail, the Incarnate Deity!
Pleased as Man with man to dwell,
Jesus, our Emmanuel!
  Hark! the herald angels sing
  Glory to the new-born King.

Hail, the heaven-born Prince of Peace!
Hail, the Sun of Righteousness!
Light and life to all He brings,
Risen with healing in His wings.
Mild He lays His glory by,
Born that man no more may die,
Born to raise the sons of earth,
Born to give them second birth.
  Hark! the herald angels sing
  Glory to the new-born King.

Varied from Charles Wesley, 1739.

71

Four 7's.

FOR Thy mercy and Thy grace,
Constant through another year,
Hear our song of thankfulness ;
Father, and Redeemer, hear.

Lo, our sins on Thee we cast,
Thee, our perfect sacrifice ;
And, forgetting all the past,
Press towards our glorious prize.

Dark the future ; let Thy light
Guide us, bright and morning Star :
Fierce our foes and hard the fight ;
Arm us, Saviour, for the war.

In our weakness and distress,
Rock of strength be Thou our stay ;
In the pathless wilderness
Be our true and living way.

Who of us death's awful road
In the coming year shall tread,
With Thy rod and staff, O God,
Comfort Thou his dying bed.

Keep us faithful, keep us pure,
Keep us evermore Thine own,
Help, O help us to endure,
Fit us for the promised crown.

So within Thy palace-gate
We shall praise on golden strings
Thee, the only Potentate,
Lord of lords, and King of kings !

Henry Downton, 1839.

72

11. 10. 11. 10.

BRIGHTEST and best of the sons of the morning,
  Dawn on our darkness and lend us Thine aid !
Star of the East, the horizon adorning,
  Guide where our infant Redeemer is laid !

Cold on His cradle the dew-drops are shining,
  Low lies His head with the beasts of the stall ;
Angels adore Him in slumber reclining,
  Maker and Monarch and Saviour of all !

Say, shall we yield Him in costly devotion
  Odours of Edom, and offerings divine,
Gems of the mountain, and pearls of the ocean,
  Myrrh from the forest, or gold from the mine ?

Vainly we offer each ample oblation,
  Vainly with gifts would His favour secure ;
Richer by far is the heart's adoration ;
  Dearer to God are the prayers of the poor.

Brightest and best of the sons of the morning,
  Dawn on our darkness and lend us Thine aid !
Star of the East, the horizon adorning
  Guide where our infant Redeemer is laid !

Bishop Heber, 1811.

73

Six 7's.

AS with gladness men of old
Did the guiding star behold ;
As with joy they hailed its light,
Leading onward, beaming bright.
So, most gracious Lord, may we
Evermore be led to Thee.

As with joyful steps they sped
To that lowly manger-bed,
There to bend the knee before
Him whom heaven and earth adore ;
So may we with willing feet
Ever seek the mercy-seat.

As they offered gifts most rare
At that manger rude and bare,
So may we with holy joy,
Pure, and free from sin's alloy,
All our costliest treasures bring,
Christ, to Thee our heavenly King.

Holy Jesus, every day
Keep us in the narrow way ;
And when earthly things are past,
Bring our ransomed souls at last
Where they need no star to guide,
Where no clouds Thy glory hide.

In the heavenly country bright
Need they no created light ;
Thou its Light, its Joy, its Crown,
Thou its Sun which goes not down ;
There for ever may we sing
Alleluias to our King.

William C. Dix, 1860.

74

8. 7. 8. 7

EARTH has many a noble city ;
  Bethlehem, thou dost all excel :
Out of thee the Lord from Heaven
  Came to rule His Israel.

Fairer than the sun at morning
  Was the star that told His birth,
To the world its God announcing,
  Seen in fleshly form on earth.

Eastern sages at His cradle
  Make oblations rich and rare ;
See them give, in deep devotion,
  Gold, and frankincense, and myrrh.

Sacred gifts of mystic meaning :
  Incense doth their God disclose,
Gold the King of kings proclaimeth,
  Myrrh His sepulchre foreshows.

Jesu, whom the Gentiles worshipped
  At Thy glad Epiphany,
Unto Thee, with God the Father
  And the Spirit, glory be.

Edward Caswall, 1849,
from the Latin of Prudentius, ✠ 413.
(Varied by compilers of Hymns A. and M., 1861.)

75

D. C. M.

O KING of Glory, David's son,
  Our Sovereign and our Friend,
In heaven for ever stands Thy throne,
  Thy kingdom hath no end :
Oh, now to all men, far and near,
  Lord, make it known, we pray,
That, as in heaven, all creatures here
  May know Thee and obey.

The Eastern sages gladly bring
  Their tribute-gifts to Thee ;
They witness that Thou art their King,
  And humbly bow the knee ;
To Thee the morning star doth lead,
  To Thee the inspired word,
We hail Thee, Saviour, in our need,
  We worship Thee, the Lord.

Oh, bid Thy word, the fairest star,
  Within us clearly shine ;
Keep sin and all false doctrine far,
  Since Thou hast claimed us Thine.
Let us Thy name aright confess,
  And with Thy Christendom
Our King and Saviour own and bless
  Through all this world to come.

Catherine Winkworth, 1858,
from the German of Behemb, 1606.

76

L. M.

O CHRIST, our true and only Light,
Illumine those who sit in night,
Let those afar now hear Thy voice,
And in Thy fold with us rejoice.

Fill with the radiance of Thy grace
The souls now lost in error's maze,
And all whom in their secret minds
Some dark delusion hurts and blinds.

And all, who else have strayed from Thee,
Oh, gently seek ! Thy healing be
To every wounded conscience given,
And let them also share Thy heaven.

Oh, make the deaf to hear Thy word,
And teach the dumb to speak, dear Lord,
Who dare not yet the faith avow,
Though secretly they hold it now.

Shine on the darkened and the cold,
Recall the wanderers from Thy fold,
Unite those now who walk apart,
Confirm the weak and doubting heart.

So they with us may evermore
Such grace with wondering thanks adore,
And endless praise to Thee be given
By all Thy Church in earth and heaven.

Catherine Winkworth, 1858,
from the German of J. Heermann, 1630.

77

Six 7's.

IS thy heart athirst to know
  That the King of heaven and earth
Deigns to dwell with man below,
  Yea, hath stooped to mortal birth?
Search the word with ceaseless care,
Till thou find this treasure there.

With the sages from afar
  Journey on o'er sea and land,
Till thou see the Morning Star
  O'er thy heart unchanging stand;
Then shalt thou behold His face
Full of mercy, truth, and grace.

For if Christ be born within,
  Soon that likeness shall appear
Which the heart had lost through sin,
  God's own image fair and clear,
And the soul serene and bright
Mirrors back His heavenly light.

Jesus, let me seek for nought
  But that Thou shouldst dwell in me;
Let this only fill my thought,
  How I may grow liker Thee,
Through this earthly care and strife,
Through the calm eternal life.

Catherine Winkworth, 1858,
from the German of Laurentius Laurenti, 1700.

78

THERE is a book, who runs may read,
  Which heavenly truth imparts,
And all the lore its scholars need
  Pure eyes and Christian hearts.

The works of God, above, below,
  Within us, and around,
Are pages in that book to show
  How God Himself is found.

The glorious sky, embracing all,
  Is like the Maker's love,
Wherewith encompassed, great and small
  In peace and order move.

The moon above, the Church below,
  A wondrous race they run ;
But all their radiance, all their glow,
  Each borrows of its sun.

One name, above all glorious names,
  With its ten thousand tongues
The everlasting sea proclaims
  Echoing angelic songs.

The raging fire, the roaring wind,
  Thy boundless power display ;
But in the gentler breeze we find
  Thy Spirit's viewless way.

Two worlds are ours : 'tis only sin
  Forbids us to descry
The mystic heaven and earth within,
  Plain as the sea and sky.

Thou, Who hast given me eyes to see
  And love this sight so fair,
Give me a heart to find out Thee
  And read Thee everywhere.

John Keble, 1819.

79

D. C. M.

O LORD, turn not Thy face away
　From them that lowly lie,
Lamenting sore their sinful life
　With tears and bitter cry !
Thy mercy-gates are open wide
　To them that mourn their sin :
O shut them not against us, Lord,
　But let us enter in !

We need not to confess our fault,
　For surely Thou canst tell ;
What we have done and what we are,
　Thou knowest very well ;
Wherefore to beg and to entreat
　With tears we come to thee,
As children that have done amiss
　Fall at their father's knee.

And need we then, O Lord, repeat
　The blessing which we crave,
When Thou dost know before we speak
　The thing that we would have ?
Mercy, O Lord, mercy we seek ;
　This is the total sum ;
For mercy, Lord, is all our prayer :
　Oh, let Thy mercy come !

Variation by Bishop Heber, 1827,
from John Mardley, 1562.

80

(Psalm LI.)

S. M.

HAVE mercy, Lord, on me,
As Thou wert ever kind,
Let me, oppressed with loads of guilt,
Thy wonted mercy find.

Wash off my foul offence,
And cleanse me from my sin ;
For I confess my crime and see
How great my guilt hath been.

Withdraw not Thou Thy help,
Nor cast me from Thy sight ;
Nor let Thy Holy Spirit take
Its everlasting flight.

The joy Thy favour gives
Let me again obtain ;
And Thy free Spirit's firm support
My fainting soul sustain.

Tate and Brady, 1696.

81

8. 8. 8. 6.

JUST as I am, without one plea
But that Thy blood was shed for me,
And that Thou bidd'st me come to Thee,
     O Lamb of God, I come.

Just as I am, though tossed about
With many a conflict, many a doubt,
Fightings and fears within, without,
     O Lamb of God, I come.

Just as I am, poor, wretched. blind ;
Sight, riches, healing of the mind,
Yea, all I need, in Thee to find,
     O Lamb of God, I come.

Just as I am, Thou wilt receive,
Wilt welcome, pardon, cleanse, relieve ;
Because Thy promise I believe,
     O Lamb of God, I come.

Just as I am (Thy love unknown
Has broken every barrier down),
Now to be Thine, yea, Thine alone,
     O Lamb of God, I come.

Just as I am, of that free love
The breadth, length, depth, and height to prove,
Here for a season, then above,
     O Lamb of God, I come.

Charlotte Elliott, 1836.

82 Eight 7's.

LORD, Thy death and passion give
  Strength and comfort at my need,
Every hour while here I live
  On Thy love my soul shall feed.
Doth some evil thought up-start?
Lo, Thy cross defends my heart,
Shows the peril, and I shrink
Back from loitering on the brink.

Would the world my steps entice
  To yon wild and level road,
Filled with mirth and pleasant vice?
  Lord I think upon the load
Thou didst once for me endure,
And I fly all thoughts impure;
Thinking on Thy bitter pains,
Hushed in prayer my heart remains.

Yes, Thy cross hath power to heal
  All the wounds of sin and strife,
Lost in Thee my heart doth feel
  Sudden warmth and nobler life.
In my saddest, darkest grief,
Let Thy sweetness bring relief,
Thou who camest but to save,
Thou who fearedst not the grave.

Lord, in Thee I place my trust,
  Thou art my defence and tower;
Death Thou treadest in the dust,
  O'er my soul he hath no power.
That I may have part in Thee
Help and save and comfort me,
Give me of Thy grace and might
Resurrection, life, and light.

Catherine Winkworth, 1855,
from the German of Heermann, 1644.

G 2

83

C. M.

O HELP us Lord ! each hour of need
  Thy heavenly succour give ;
Help us in thought, and word, and deed,
  Each hour on earth we live !

O help us when our spirits bleed,
  With contrite anguish sore ;
And when our hearts are cold and dead,
  Oh, help us, Lord, the more !

O help us, through the prayer of faith,
  More firmly to believe ;
For still, the more the servant hath,
  The more shall he receive.

O help us, Jesus, from on high !
  We know no help but Thee :
O help us so to live and die,
  As Thine in heaven to be !

Henry H. Milman, 1827.

84

L. M.

O THOU, to whose all-searching sight
The darkness shineth as the light,
Try us, and prove our treacherous heart,
And bid the power of sin depart.

As through this vale of tears we stray,
Be Thou our light, be Thou our stay ;
Mark out the pilgrim's heavenly road,
That leads us to the mount of God.

If storms and tempests cloud our way,
Our strength proportion to our day ;
Nor storms nor tempests need we fear,
If Thou, our sun and shield, be near.

Guide and uphold us with Thy hand,
Till we arrive at Canaan's land ;
The land where sin and death shall cease,
The land of rest, and joy, and peace.

John Wesley, 1743,
from the German.

85

Eight 7's.

JESU, lover of my soul,
  Let me to Thy bosom fly,
While the nearer waters roll,
  While the tempest still is high.
Hide me, O my Saviour, hide,
  Till the storm of life be past:
Safe into the haven guide !
  O receive my soul at last !

Other refuge have I none,
  Hangs my helpless soul on Thee ;
Leave, O leave me not alone ;
  Still support and comfort me !
All my hope on Thee is stayed ;
  All my help from Thee I bring :
Cover my defenceless head
  With the shadow of Thy wing !

Plenteous grace with Thee is found,
  Grace to cover all my sin ;
Let the healing streams abound ;
  Make and keep me pure within !
Thou of life the fountain art,
  Freely let me take of Thee :
Spring Thou up within my heart,
  Rise to all eternity !

Charles Wesley, 1740.

86

C. M.

O THOU from Whom all goodness flows,
  I lift my heart to Thee ;
In all my sorrows, conflicts, woes,
  Good Lord, remember me.

When on my fearful burdened heart
  My sins lie heavily,
Thy pardon grant, Thy peace impart :
  In love remember me.

When trials sore obstruct my way,
  And ills I cannot flee,
O let my strength be as my day :
  Good Lord, remember me.

If on my face, for Thy dear name,
  Shame and reproaches be,
All hail reproach, and welcome shame,
  If Thou remember me.

When in the solemn hour of death
  I wait Thy just decree,
" Saviour," with my last parting breath
  I'll cry, " Remember me."

And when before Thy throne I stand,
  And lift my eyes to Thee,
Then, with the saints at Thy right hand,
  Receive and pardon me.

Thomas Haweis, 1792.

87

Six 8's.

WHEN gathering clouds around I view,
And days are dark, and friends are few,
On Him I lean, who not in vain
Experienced every human pain ;
He sees my wants, allays my fears,
And counts and treasures up my tears.

If aught should tempt my soul to stray
From heavenly wisdom's narrow way,
To fly the good I would pursue,
Or do the sin I would not do,
Still He, who felt temptation's power,
Shall guard me in that dangerous hour.

If vexing thoughts within me rise,
And sore dismayed my spirit dies,
Still He, who once vouchsafed to bear
The sickening anguish of despair,
Shall sweetly soothe, shall gently dry,
The throbbing heart, the streaming eye.

And O ! when I have safely past
Through every conflict but the last,
Still, still, unchanging, watch beside
My painful bed, for Thou hast died ;
Then point to realms of cloudless day,
And wipe the latest tear away.

Sir Robert Grant, 1812.

88

7. 7. 7. 5.

LORD of mercy and of might,
Of mankind the Life and Light,
Maker, Teacher, Infinite,
   Jesus ! hear and save !

Who, when sin's tremendous doom
Gave creation to the tomb,
Didst not scorn the Virgin's womb,
   Jesus ! hear and save !

Mighty monarch ! Saviour mild !
Humbled to a mortal child,
Captive, beaten, bound, reviled,
   Jesus ! hear and save !

Throned above celestial things,
Borne aloft on angels' wings,
Lord of lords, and King of kings,
   Jesus ! hear and save !

Who shalt yet return from high,
Robed in might and majesty,
Hear us, help us when we cry !
   Jesus ! hear and save !

Bishop Heber, 1812.

89

Six 7's

FORTH from the dark and stormy sky,
Lord, to Thine altar's shade we fly;
Forth from the world, its hope and fear,
Saviour, we seek Thy shelter here;
Weary and weak, Thy grace we pray;
Turn not Thy suppliants, Lord, away!

Long have we roamed in want and pain,
Long have we sought Thy rest in vain:
Wandering in doubt, in darkness lost,
Long have our souls been tempest-tost!
Low at Thy feet our sins we lay;
Turn not Thy suppliants, Lord, away!

Bishop Heber, 1827.

90

6. 6. 4. 6. 6. 6. 4.

MY faith looks up to Thee,
Thou Lamb of Calvary,
  Saviour divine !
Now hear me while I pray ;
Take all my guilt away ;
O let me from this day
  Be wholly Thine !

May Thy rich grace impart
Strength to my fainting heart,
  My zeal inspire !
As Thou hast died for me,
O may my love to Thee
Pure, warm, and changeless be,
  A living fire !

While life's dark maze I tread,
And griefs around me spread,
  Be Thou my Guide !
Bid darkness turn to day,
Wipe sorrow's tears away,
Nor let me ever stray
  From Thee aside.

When ends life's transient dream,
When death's cold sullen stream
  Shall o'er me roll ;
Blest Saviour ! then in love
Fear and distrust remove ;
O bear me safe above,
  A ransomed soul !

Ray Palmer, 1830.

91

L. M.

"TAKE up the Cross," the Saviour said,
" If thou wouldst my disciple be ;
" Deny thyself, the world forsake,
"And humbly follow after Me."

Take up the Cross ; let not its weight
Fill thy weak spirit with alarm :
His strength shall bear thy spirit up,
And brace thy heart, and nerve thine arm.

Take up the Cross, nor heed the shame,
Nor let thy foolish pride rebel :
Thy Lord for thee the Cross endured
To save thy soul from death and hell.

Take up the Cross, then, in His strength,
And calmly every danger brave ;
It guides thee to a better home,
And gives thee victory o'er the grave.

Take up the Cross, and follow Christ,
Nor think till death to lay it down ;
For only he who bears the Cross
May hope to win and wear the crown.

Charles W. Everest, 1833.

92

C. M.

LORD, as to Thy dear Cross we flee,
  And plead to be forgiven,
So let Thy life our pattern be,
  And form our souls for heaven.

Help us through good report and ill
  Our daily cross to bear,
Like Thee to do our Father's will,
  Our brethren's griefs to share.

Let grace our selfishness expel,
  Our earthliness refine,
And kindness in our bosoms dwell,
  As free and true as Thine.

If joy should at Thy bidding fly,
  And grief's dark day come on,
We in our turn would meekly cry,
  " Father, Thy will be done ! "

Kept peaceful in the midst of strife,
  Forgiving and forgiven,
O may we lead the pilgrim's life,
  And follow Thee to heaven !

John H. Gurney, 1838.

93

8. 8. 8. 6.

O THOU, the contrite sinners' Friend,
Who loving, lov'st them to the end,
On this alone my hopes depend,
    That Thou wilt plead for me !

When, weary in the Christian race,
Far off appears my resting-place,
And fainting I mistrust Thy grace,
    Then, Saviour, plead for me !

When I have erred and gone astray
Afar from Thine and wisdom's way,
And see no glimmering, guiding ray,
    Still, Saviour, plead for me !

When Satan, by my sins made bold,
Strives from Thy Cross to loose my hold,
Then with Thy pitying arms enfold,
    And plead, O plead for me !

And when my dying hour draws near,
Darkened with anguish, guilt, and fear,
Then to my fainting sight appear,
    Pleading in heaven for me !

When the full light of heavenly day
Reveals my sins in dread array,
Say Thou hast washed them all away ;
    O say, Thou plead'st for me !

Charlotte Elliott, 1833.

94

D. 6. 5. 6. 5.

IN the hour of trial,
  Jesu ! pray for me,
Lest by base denial
  I depart from Thee :
When Thou seest me waver,
  With a look recall,
Nor, for fear or favour,
  Suffer me to fall.

With forbidden pleasures
  Should this vain world charm,
Or its tempting treasures
  Spread to work me harm,
Bring to my remembrance
  Sad Gethsemane,
Or, in darker semblance,
  Cross-crowned Calvary.

Should Thy mercy send me
  Sorrow, toil, and woe ;
Or should pain attend me
  On my path below ;
Grant that I may never
  Fail Thy hand to see ;
Grant that I may ever
  Cast my care on Thee.

When my last hour cometh,
  Fraught with strife and pain,
When my dust returneth
  To the dust again ;
On Thy truth relying
  Through that mortal strife,
Jesu ! take me, dying,
  To eternal life.

James Montgomery, 1853.

95

HEAL me, O my Saviour, heal ;
Heal me as I suppliant kneel ;
Heal me, and my pardon seal.

Fresh the wounds that sin hath made ;
Hear the prayers I oft have prayed,
And in mercy send me aid.

Thou the true physician art :
Thou, O Christ, canst health impart,
Binding up the bleeding heart.

Other comforters are gone ;
Thou canst heal, and Thou alone,
Thou for all my sin atone.

Heal me then, my Saviour, heal ;
Heal me as I suppliant kneel :
To Thy mercy I appeal.

Godfrey Thring, 1866.

96

SON of Man, to Thee we cry ;
By the wondrous mystery
Of Thy dwelling here on earth,
By Thy pure and holy birth,
Lord, Thy presence let us see,
Thou our Light and Saviour be !

Lamb of God, to Thee we cry ;
By Thy bitter agony,
By Thy pangs, to us unknown,
By Thy spirit's parting groan,
Lord, Thy presence let us see,
Thou our Light and Saviour be !

Prince of Life, to Thee we cry ;
By Thy glorious majesty,
By Thy triumph o'er the grave,
By Thy power to help and save,
Lord, Thy presence let us see,
Thou our Light and Saviour be !

Lord of Glory, God most high,
Man exalted to the sky,
With Thy love our bosom fill ;
Help us to perform Thy will ;
Then Thy glory we shall see,
Thou wilt bring us home to Thee.

Bishop Mant, 1837.

H

97

Three 7's.

LORD, in this Thy mercy's day,
Ere it pass for aye away,
On our knees we fall and pray.

Holy Jesu, grant us tears,
Fill us with heart-searching fears,
Ere the hour of doom appears.

Lord, on us Thy Spirit pour,
Kneeling lowly at the door,
Ere it close for evermore.

By Thy night of agony,
By Thy supplicating cry,
By Thy willingness to die,

By Thy tears of bitter woe
For Jerusalem below,
Let us not Thy love forego.

Grant us 'neath Thy wings a place,
Lest we lose this day of grace,
Ere we shall behold Thy face.

Isaac Williams, 1844.

98

L. M.

RIDE on ! ride on in majesty !
Hark ! all the tribes Hosanna cry;
O Saviour meek, pursue Thy road,
With palms and scattered garments strowed.

Ride on ! ride on in majesty !
In lowly pomp ride on to die :
O Christ, Thy triumphs now begin
O'er captive death and conquered sin.

Ride on ! ride on in majesty !
The angel armies of the sky
Look down with sad and wondering eyes
To see the approaching Sacrifice.

Ride on ! ride on in majesty !
Thy last and fiercest strife is nigh :
The Father on His sapphire throne
Awaits His own anointed Son.

Ride on ! ride on in majesty !
In lowly pomp ride on to die :
Bow Thy meek head to mortal pain,
Then take, O God, Thy power, and reign.

Henry H. Milman, 1827.

99

Four 8's.

HOSANNA to the living Lord !
Hosanna to the incarnate Word !
To Christ, Creator, Saviour, King,
Let earth, let heaven, Hosanna sing.

" Hosanna," Lord, Thine angels cry :
" Hosanna," Lord, Thy saints reply :
Above, beneath us, and around,
The dead and living swell the sound.

O Saviour, with protecting care
Return to this Thy house of prayer,
Assembled in Thy sacred Name,
Where we Thy parting promise claim.

But, chiefest, in our cleansèd breast,
Eternal, bid Thy Spirit rest ;
And make our secret soul to be
A temple pure, and worthy Thee.

So in the last and dreadful day,
When earth and heaven shall melt away,
Thy flock, redeemed from sinful stain,
Shall swell the sound of praise again.

Bishop Heber, 1811

100

Eight 7's.

SAVIOUR, when in dust to Thee
Low we bow the adoring knee—
When, repentant, to the skies
Scarce we lift our weeping eyes—
Oh, by all the pains and woe,
Suffered once for man below,
Bending from Thy throne on high,
Hear our solemn Litany !

By Thy helpless infant years ;
By Thy life of want and tears ;
By Thy days of sore distress
In the savage wilderness ;
By the dread mysterious hour
Of the insulting tempter's power :
Turn, oh, turn a favouring eye,
Hear our solemn Litany !

By Thine hour of dire despair ;
By Thine agony of prayer ;
By the cross, the nail, the thorn,
Piercing spear, and torturing scorn ;
By the gloom that veiled the skies
O'er the dreadful sacrifice ;
Listen to our humble cry,
Hear our solemn Litany !

By Thy deep expiring groan ;
By the sad sepulchral stone ;
By the vault whose dark abode
Held in vain the rising God ;
Oh, from earth to heaven restored,
Mighty re-ascended Lord,
Listen, listen, to the cry
Of our solemn Litany !

Sir Robert Grant, 1815.

101

Four 7's.

WHEN our heads are bowed with woe,
When our bitter tears o'erflow,
When we mourn the lost, the dear,
Gracious Son of Mary, hear !

Thou our throbbing flesh hast worn,
Thou our mortal griefs hast borne,
Thou hast shed the human tear :
Gracious Son of Mary, hear !

When the heart is sad within
With the thought of all its sin ;
When the spirit shrinks with fear,
Gracious Son of Mary, hear !

Thou the shame, the grief hast known,
Though the sins were not Thine own,
Thou hast deigned their load to bear :
Gracious Son of Mary, hear !

When the solemn death-bell tolls
For our frail departed souls,
When our final doom is near,
Jesu, Son of Mary, hear !

Thou hast bowed the dying head,
Thou the atoning blood hast shed,
Thou hast risen from the grave ;
Holy Jesus, hear and save !

Henry H. Milman, 1827.

102

Six 7's.

GO to dark Gethsemane,
  Ye who feel the tempter's power ;
Your Redeemer's conflict see,
  Watch with Him one bitter hour :
Turn not from His griefs away,
Learn from Him to watch and pray.

See Him at the judgment-hall,
  Beaten, bound, reviled, arraigned ;
See Him meekly bearing all—
  Love to man His soul sustained :
Shun not suffering, shame, or loss ;
Learn of Christ to bear the cross.

Calvary's mournful mountain view ;
  There the Lord of Glory see,
Made a sacrifice for you,
  Dying on the accursèd tree :
" It is finished," hear Him cry,
Trust in Christ, and learn to die.

Early to the tomb repair,
  Where they laid His breathless clay ;
Angels kept their vigils there—
  Who hath taken Him away ?
Christ is risen, He seeks the skies :
Saviour ! teach us so to rise.

James Montgomery, 1822.

103

Six 7's.

ROCK of Ages, cleft for me,
Let me hide myself in Thee ;
Let the water and the blood,
From Thy riven side which flowed,
Be of sin the double cure—
Save from wrath, and make me pure.

Nothing in my hand I bring,
Simply to Thy cross I cling:
Could my zeal no languor know,
Could my tears for ever flow,
All for sin could not atone ;
Thou must save, and Thou alone.

While I draw this fleeting breath,
When my eyelids close in death,
When I rise to worlds unknown,
See Thee on Thy judgment Throne,
Rock of Ages, cleft for me,
Let me hide myself in Thee.

Augustus M. Toplady, 1776.

104

D. 7. 6. 7. 6.

O SACRED Head, surrounded
  By crown of piercing thorn !
O bleeding Head, so wounded,
  Reviled, and put to scorn !
Death's pallid hue comes o'er Thee,
  The glow of life decays,
Yet angel-hosts adore Thee,
  And tremble as they gaze.

I see Thy strength and vigour
  All fading in the strife,
And death with cruel rigour
  Bereaving Thee of life ;
O agony and dying !
  O love to sinners free !
Jesu, all grace supplying,
  Oh, turn Thy face on me.

In this Thy bitter passion,
  Good Shepherd, think of me
With Thy most sweet compassion,
  Unworthy though I be :
Beneath Thy Cross abiding
  For ever would I rest ;
In Thy dear love confiding,
  And with Thy presence blest.

Sir Henry W. Baker, 1861,
from the Latin of St. Bernard, ✠ 1153.

105

D. 8. 8. 7.

BY the Cross sad vigil keeping,
Stood the Mother, mournful, weeping,
　　Where her Son extended hung :
And the piercing sword, deep driven,
Hath aghast and sorrow-riven
　　All her soul, with anguish wrung.

Make me weep beside Thee ever ;
From Thy Cross may nought dissever
　　Me, so long as I shall live ;
Near it let me stand and sorrow,
Hallowing many a mournful morrow
　　With the tears that Thou shalt give.

There, by Thy blest Mother bending,
Tears with tears so holy blending,
　　Let me in her anguish share :
Let me, every lust denying,
Feel within my Saviour's dying,
　　Of Thy wounds some impress bear.

Jesu, may Thy Cross defend me,
Through Thy death salvation send me,
　　Shield me with Thy grace and love !
When death severs flesh and spirit,
May my soul through Thee inherit
　　Thy bright paradise above !

Variation from Bishop Mant's translation (1837)
of the "Stabat Mater Dolorosa," of Jacobus
de Benedictis, ✠ 1306.

106

L. M.

WHEN I survey the wondrous Cross
  On which the Prince of Glory died,
My richest gain I count but loss,
  And pour contempt on all my pride.

Forbid it, Lord, that I should boast
  Save in the death of Christ, my God ;
All the vain things that charm me most
  I sacrifice them to His blood.

See from His head, His hands, His feet,
  Sorrow and love flow mingled down ;
Did e'er such love and sorrow meet,
  Or thorns compose so rich a crown ?

Were the whole realm of nature mine,
  That were a present far too small ;
Love so amazing, so divine,
  Demands my soul, my life, my all.

Isaac Watts, 1709.

107

8. 7. 8. 7. 7. 7.

ALL is o'er : the pain, the sorrow,
  Human taunts, and fiendish spite :
Death shall be despoiled to-morrow
  Of the prey he grasps to-night.
Yet once more, His own to save,
Christ must sleep within the grave.

Close and still the cell that holds Him,
  While in brief repose He lies ;
Deep the slumber that enfolds Him
  Veiled a while from mortal eyes —
Slumber such as needs must be
After hard-won victory.

Fierce and deadly was the anguish,
  When the bitter cross He bore ;
How did soul and body languish,
  Till the toil of death was o'er !
But that toil, so fierce and dread,
Bruised and crushed the serpent's head.

So this night, with voice of sadness,
  Chant His requiem soft and low ;
Loftier strains of praise and gladness
  From to-morrow's harps shall flow :
Death and hell at length are slain—
Christ hath triumphed, Christ doth reign !

John Moultrie, 1822.

108

L. M.

LORD Jesus, who, our souls to save,
Did'st rest and slumber in the grave,
Now grant us all in Thee to rest,
And here to live as seems Thee best.

Give us the strength, the dauntless faith,
That Thou hast purchased with Thy death,
And lead us to that glorious place
Where we shall see the Father's face.

'O Lamb of God ! who once wast slain,
We thank Thee for that bitter pain !
Let us partake Thy death, that we
May enter into life with Thee.

Catherine Winkworth, 1858,
from the German of G. Werner, 1638.

109

7. 4. 7. 4.

JESUS Christ is risen to-day,   Hallelujah !
Our triumphant holy-day,   Hallelujah !
Who did once upon the cross   Hallelujah !
Suffer to redeem our loss.   Hallelujah !

Hymns of praise then let us sing   Hallelujah !
Unto Christ our heavenly King,   Hallelujah !
Who endured the cross and grave   Hallelujah !
Sinners to redeem and save !   Hallelujah !

But the pains which He endured   Hallelujah !
Our salvation have procured :   Hallelujah !
Now He reigns above the sky,   Hallelujah !
Where the angels ever cry,   Hallelujah !

Anon. 1750.

I IO

Four 7's.

CHRIST the Lord is risen to-day,
Sons of men and angels say ;
Raise your joys and triumphs high :
Sing, ye heavens, and, earth, reply.

Love's redeeming work is done ;
Fought the fight, the battle won :
Lo, our Sun's eclipse is o'er ;
Lo, He sets in blood no more !

Vain the stone, the watch, the seal ;
Christ hath burst the gates of hell :
Death in vain forbids His rise ;
Christ hath opened Paradise !

Lives again our glorious King !
Where, O Death, is now thy sting ?
Once He died, our souls to save ;
Where's thy victory, O Grave ?

Soar we now where Christ hath led,
Following our exalted Head ;
Made like Him, like Him we rise ;
Ours the cross, the grave, the skies.

King of glory, King of bliss,
Everlasting life is this—
Thee to know, Thy power to prove,
Thee to sing, and Thee to love.

Charles Wesley, 1743.

I I I

Three 8's.

THE strife is o'er, the battle done ;
The triumph of the Lord is won ;
O let the song of praise be sung,

Alleluia !

The powers of death have done their worst,
And Jesus hath His foes dispersed ;
Let shouts of praise and joy outburst,

Alleluia !

On that third morn He rose again
In glorious majesty to reign ;
O let us swell the joyful strain,

Alleluia !

He closed the yawning gates of hell ;
The bars from heaven's high portals fell ;
Let songs of joy His triumphs tell,

Alleluia !

Lord, by the stripes which wounded Thee,
From death's dread sting Thy servants free,
That we may live and sing to Thee

Alleluia !

Francis Pott, 1860,
from a Latin hymn of twelfth century.

112

P. M.

JESUS lives ! no longer now
  Can thy terrors, Death, appal us :
Jesus lives ! by this we know
  Thou, O Grave, canst not enthral us.
                Hallelujah !

Jesus lives ! henceforth is death
  But the gate of life immortal ;
This shall calm our trembling breath,
  When we pass its gloomy portal.
                Hallelujah !

Jesus lives ! for us He died ;
  Then alone to Jesus living,
Pure in heart may we abide,
  Glory to our Saviour giving.
                Hallelujah !

Jesus lives ! our hearts know well
  Nought from us His love shall sever,
Life, nor death, nor powers of hell
  Tear us from His keeping ever.
                Hallelujah !

Jesus lives ! to Him the throne
  Over all the world is given !
May we go where He is gone,
  Rest and reign with Him in heaven.
                Hallelujah !

Frances E. Cox, 1841,
from the German of C. F. Gellert, 1757.

I

113

P. M.

IN the bonds of death He lay,
  Who for our offence was slain,
But the Lord is risen to-day,
  Christ hath brought us life again !
Wherefore let us all rejoice,
Singing loud with cheerful voice,
               Hallelujah !

On this day most blest of days,
  Let us keep high festival,
For our God hath showed His grace,
  And our Sun hath risen on all,
And our hearts rejoice to see
Sin and night before Him flee.
               Hallelujah !

To the supper of the Lord
  Gladly will we come to-day,
The word of peace is now restored,
  The old leaven is put away ;
Christ will be our food alone,
Faith no life but His doth own.
               Hallelujah !

Catherine Winkworth, 1855,
from the German of Martin Luther, 1524.

114

Six 7's.

JESUS our Redeemer lives,
　Christ our trust is dead no more ;
In the strength this knowledge gives
　Shall not all our fears be o'er,
Though the night of death be fraught
Still with many an anxious thought ?

Jesus our Redeemer lives,
　And His life we once shall see ;
Bright the hope this promise gives,
　Where He is we too shall be.
Shall we fear then ? Can the Head
Rise, and leave the members dead ?

Close to Him our souls are bound
　In the bonds of hope enclasped ;
Faith's strong hand this hold hath found,
　And the Rock hath firmly grasped :
And no ban of death can part
From our Lord the trusting heart.

Only see ye that your heart
　Rise betimes from earthly lust ;
Would ye there with Him have part,
　Here obey your Lord, and trust ;
Fix your hearts beyond the skies,
Whither ye yourselves would rise.

Catherine Winkworth, 1855,
from the German of Louisa Henrietta,
Electress of Brandenburgh, 1653.

I 2

115

Four 7's.

CHRIST the Lord is risen again !
Christ hath broken every chain !
Hark, the angels shout for joy,
Singing evermore on high,

Hallelujah !

He, who gave for us His life,
Who for us endured the strife,
Is our Paschal Lamb to-day !
We too sing for joy and say,

Hallelujah !

He, who bore all pain and loss
Comfortless upon the cross,
Lives in glory now on high,
Pleads for us and hears our cry :

Hallelujah !

He, who slumbered in the grave,
Is exalted now to save ;
Now through Christendom it rings
That the Lamb is King of kings !

Hallelujah !

Now He bids us tell abroad
How the lost may be restored,
How the penitent forgiven,
How we too may enter heaven.

Hallelujah !

Thou our Paschal Lamb indeed,
Christ, to-day Thy people feed ;
Take our sins and guilt away,
Let us sing by night and day,

Hallelujah !

Catherine Winkworth, 1858,
from Michael Weiss' German translation, 1531,
from the Bohemian Brethren, 1504.

116

Four 7's.

HAIL the day that sees Him rise
Glorious to His native skies !
Christ, a while to mortals given,
Enters now the highest heaven.

There the glorious triumph waits ;
Lift your heads, eternal gates !
Christ has vanquished death and sin,
Take the King of Glory in.

Lo, the heaven its Lord receives,
Yet He loves the earth He leaves ;
Though returning to His throne,
Still He calls mankind His own.

Oh, though parted from our sight,
Far above the azure height,
Grant our hearts may thither rise,
Seeking Thee above the skies.

Ever upward let us move,
Wafted on the wings of love ;
Looking when our Lord shall come,
Longing, yearning after home.

There we shall with Thee remain
Partners of Thy endless reign,
There Thy face unclouded see,
Find our Heaven of heavens in Thee.

Charles Wesley, 1739.

117

C. M.

THE eternal gates lift up their heads,
  The doors are opened wide ;
The King of Glory is gone up
  Unto His Father's side.

Thou art gone in before us, Lord,
  Thou hast prepared a place,
That we may be where now Thou art,
  And look upon Thy face.

And ever on our earthly path
  A gleam of glory lies ;
A light still breaks behind the cloud
  That veils Thee from our eyes.

Lift up our hearts, lift up our minds,
  And let Thy grace be given,
That, while we linger yet below,
  Our treasure be in heaven :

That, where Thou art at God's right hand,
  Our hope, our love, may be :
Dwell in us now, that we may dwell
  For evermore in Thee.

Cecil F. Alexander, 1858.

118

D. S. M.

THOU art gone up on high,
To mansions in the skies ;
And round Thy throne unceasingly
The songs of praise arise ;
But we are lingering here,
With sin and care opprest :
Lord, send Thy promised Comforter,
And lead us to Thy rest.

Thou art gone up on high ;
But Thou didst first come down,
Through earth's most bitter agony
To pass unto Thy crown ;
And girt with griefs and fears
Our onward course must be ;
But only let that path of tears
Lead us at last to Thee.

Thou art gone up on high ;
But Thou shalt come again,
With all the bright ones of the sky
Attendant in Thy train.
Oh, by Thy saving power,
So make us live and die,
That we may stand in that dread hour
At Thy right hand on high !

Emma Toke, 1851.

119

PART I.   Eight 7's.

HE is gone—beyond the skies
A cloud receives Him from our eyes;
Gone beyond the highest height
Of mortal gaze or angels' flight;
Through the veils of time and space,
Passed into the Holiest place;
All the toil, the sorrow done,
All the battle fought and won.

He is gone—and we return,
And our hearts within us burn:
Olivet no more shall greet
With welcome shout His coming feet;
Never shall we track Him more
On Gennesareth's glistening shore;
Never in that look or voice
Shall Zion's hill again rejoice.

He is gone—and we remain
In this world of sin and pain;
In the void which He has left
On this earth, of Him bereft;
We have still His work to do,
We can still His path pursue;
Seek him both in friend and foe,
In ourselves His image show.

He is gone—we heard Him say,
"Good that I should go away."
Gone is that dear Form and Face,
But not gone His present grace!
Though Himself no more we see,
Comfortless we cannot be—
No! His Spirit still is ours,
Quickening, freshening, all our powers.

119

PART II.

Eight 7's.

HE is gone—towards their goal
World and Church must onward roll ;
Far behind we leave the past ;
Forwards are our glances cast :
Still His words before us range
Through the ages, as they change ;
Wheresoe'er the Truth shall lead,
He will give whate'er we need.

He is gone—but we once more
Shall behold Him as before ;
In the Heaven of heavens the same
As on earth He went and came.
In the many mansions there
Place for us He will prepare :
In that world, unseen, unknown,
He and we may yet be one.

He is gone—but not in vain ;
Wait until He comes again :
He is risen, He is not here,
Far above this earthly sphere ;
Evermore, in heart and mind,
There our peace in Him we find ;
To our own Eternal Friend
Thitherward let us ascend.

Arthur P. Stanley, 1862, ✠ 1881.

I20

7. 6. 7. 6.

DRAW us to Thee, Lord Jesus,
  And we will hasten on ;
For strong desire doth seize us
  To go where Thou art gone.

Draw us to Thee : enlighten
  These hearts to find Thy way,
That else the tempests frighten,
  Or pleasures lure astray.

Draw us to Thee ; and teach us
  E'en now that rest to find,
Where sorrow cannot reach us,
  Nor care weigh down the mind.

Draw us to Thee ; nor leave us
  Till all our path is trod ;
Then in Thy arms receive us,
  And bear us home to God.

*Catherine Winkworth, 1862,
from the German of Ludamilia Elisabeth,
Countess of Schwarzburg-Rudolstadt, 1687.*

121

Six 7's.

HEAVENWARD stretch, my soul, thy wings,
  Heavenly nature canst thou claim,
There is nought of earthly things
  Worthy to be all thine aim ;
Every soul that God inspires
Back to Him, its Source, aspires.

Heavenward ever would I haste,
  When Thy table, Lord, is spread :
Heavenly strength on earth I taste,
  Feeding on the living Bread ;
Such is e'en on earth our fare
Who Thy marriage feast shall share.

Heavenward death shall lead at last
  To the home where I would be ;
All my sorrows overpast,
  I shall triumph there with Thee,
Jesus, who hast gone before,
That we too might heavenward soar.

Heavenward, heavenward ! Only this
  Is my watchword on the earth ;
For the love of heavenly bliss
  Counting all things little worth.
Heavenward all my being tends,
Till in heaven my journey ends.

Catherine Winkworth, 1855,
from the German of Benjamin Schmolck, 1731.

122

L. M.

COME, Holy Ghost, our souls inspire,
And lighten with celestial fire ;
Thou the anointing Spirit art,
Who dost Thy sevenfold gifts impart.

Thy blessed unction from above
Is comfort, life, and fire of love ;
Enable with perpetual light
The dulness of our blinded sight.

Anoint and cheer our soilèd face
With the abundance of Thy grace ;
Keep far our foes, give peace at home ;
Where Thou art guide, no ill can come.

Teach us to know the Father, Son,
And Thee of both to be but One :
That through the ages all along
This may be our endless song,
Praise to Thy eternal merit,
Father, Son, and Holy Spirit !

Bishop Cosin, 1662,
from the " Veni, Creator Spiritus," eleventh century.

123

L. M.

COME, gracious Spirit, heavenly Dove,
With light and comfort from above ;
Be Thou our guardian, Thou our guide ;
O'er every thought and step preside.

The light of truth to us display,
And make us know and choose Thy way :
Plant holy fear in every heart,
That we from God may ne'er depart.

Lead us to holiness—the road
That we must take to dwell with God ;
Lead us to Christ, the living Way,
Nor let us from His precepts stray.

Lead us to God, our final rest,
To be with Him for ever blest ;
Lead us to heaven, its bliss to share,
Fulness of joy for ever there.

Adapted from Simon Browne, 1720.

124

L. M.

SPIRIT of mercy, truth, and love,
O shed Thine influence from above ;
And still from age to age convey
The wonders of this sacred day.

In every clime, by every tongue,
Be God's surpassing glory sung,
Let all the listening earth be taught
The acts our great Redeemer wrought.

Unfailing Comfort, Heavenly Guide,
Still o'er Thy holy Church preside ;
Still let mankind Thy blessings prove,
Spirit of mercy, truth, and love.

Anon. 1775.

125

C. M.

WHEN God of old came down from heaven
  In power and wrath He came ;
Before His feet the clouds were riven,
  Half darkness and half flame.

So when the Spirit of our God
  Came down His flock to find,
A voice from heaven was heard abroad,
  A rushing, mighty wind.

It fills the Church of God ; it fills
  The sinful world around ;
Only in stubborn hearts and wills
  No place for it is found.

Come Lord, come Wisdom, Love, and Power,
  Open our ears to hear ;
Let us not miss the accepted hour ;
  Save, Lord, by love or fear.

John Keble, 1827.

126

8. 6. 8. 4.

OUR blest Redeemer, ere He breathed
  His tender last farewell,
A Guide, a Comforter bequeathed
  With us to dwell.

He came sweet influence to impart,
  A gracious, willing Guest,
While He can find one humble heart
  Wherein to rest.

And His that gentle voice we hear,
  Soft as the breath of even,
That checks each thought, that calms each fear,
  And speaks of heaven.

And every virtue we possess,
  And every conquest won,
And every thought of holiness,
  Are His alone.

Spirit of purity and grace,
  Our weakness, pitying, see:
Oh, make our hearts Thy dwelling place,
  And meet for Thee!

Harriet Auber, 1829.

127

L. M.

SPIRIT of God, that moved of old
  Upon the waters' darkened face,
Come, when our faithless hearts are cold,
  And stir them with an inward grace! ·

Thou, that art Power and Peace combined,
  All highest Strength, all purest Love,
The rushing of the mighty wind,
  The brooding of the gentle dove,

O give us still Thy powerful aid,
  And urge us on, and keep us Thine ;
Nor leave the hearts that once were made
  Fit temples for Thy grace divine.

Nor let us quench Thy sevenfold light :
  But still with softest breathings stir
Our wayward souls, and lead us right,
  O Holy Ghost, our Comforter !

Cecil F. Alexander, 1858.

K

128

Three 7's.

HOLY GHOST! my Comforter!
Now from highest heaven appear;
Shed Thy gracious radiance here.

Come, in Thee our toil is sweet,
Shelter from the noonday heat,
From whom sorrow flieth fleet!

What without Thy aid is wrought,
Skilful deed or wisest thought,
God will count but vain and nought.

Bend the stubborn will to Thine,
Melt the cold with fire divine,
Erring hearts aright incline.

Grant us, Lord, who cry to Thee,
Steadfast in Thy faith to be :
Give Thy gifts of charity.

May we live in holiness,
And in death find happiness,
And abide with Thee in bliss!

*Catherine Winkworth, 1862,
from a German translation of the seventeenth
century.*

129

Eight 8's.

COME, Holy Spirit, God and Lord,
Be all Thy graces now outpoured
On the believer's mind and soul,
And touch our hearts with living coal.
Thy light this day shone forth so clear,
All tongues and nations gathered near,
To learn that faith for which we bring
Glad praise to Thee, and loudly sing.

Thou strong Defence, Thou holy Light,
Teach us to know our God aright,
And call him Father from the heart :
The word of life and truth impart,
That we may love not doctrines strange,
Nor e'er to other teachers range,
But Jesus for our Master own
And put our trust in Him alone.

Thou sacred Ardour, Comfort sweet,
Help us to wait with ready feet
And willing heart at Thy command,
Nor trial fright us from Thy band.
Lord, make us ready with Thy powers,
Strengthen the flesh in weaker hours,
That as good warriors we may force
Through life and death to Thee our course.

*Catherine Winkworth, 1855,
from the German of Martin Luther, 1524.*

P. M.

HOLY, holy, holy, Lord God Almighty !
Early in the morning our song shall rise to Thee ;
Holy, holy, holy, merciful and mighty !
God in Three Persons, blessed Trinity !

Holy, holy, holy ! all the saints adore Thee,
Casting down their golden crowns around the glassy
    sea ;
Cherubim and Seraphim falling down before Thee,
Which wert, and art, and evermore shalt be !

Holy, holy, holy ! though the darkness hide Thee,
Though the eye of sinful man Thy glory may not see ;
Only Thou art holy, there is none beside Thee
Perfect in power, in love and purity !

Holy, holy, holy, Lord God Almighty !
All Thy works shall praise Thy name in earth, and
    sky, and sea :
Holy, holy, holy, merciful and mighty !
God in Three Persons, blessed Trinity !

Bishop Heber, 1827.

131

7. 7. 7. 5.

THREE in One, and One in Three,
Ruler of the earth and sea,
Hear us while we lift to Thee
    Holy chant and psalm.

Light of lights ! with morning shine ;
Lift on us Thy light divine ;
And let charity benign
    Breathe on us her balm.

Light of lights ! when falls the even,
Let it close on sins forgiven ;
Fold us in the peace of heaven,
    Shed a holy calm.

Three in One, and One in Three,
Dimly here we worship Thee ;
With the saints hereafter we
    Hope to bear the palm.

Gilbert Rorison, 1850,
based on two Latin hymns.

132

L. M.

FATHER of heaven, whose love profound
A ransom for our souls hath found,
Before Thy throne we sinners bend ;
To us Thy pardoning love extend !

Almighty Son, incarnate Word !
Our Prophet, Priest, Redeemer, Lord !
Before Thy throne we sinners bend ;
To us Thy saving grace extend !

Eternal Spirit ! by whose breath
The soul is raised from sin and death,
Before Thy throne we sinners bend ;
To us Thy quickening power extend !

Jehovah, Father, Spirit, Son—
Mysterious Godhead, Three in One !
Before Thy throne we sinners bend ;
Grace, pardon, life, to us extend !

J. Cooper, 1810.

133

(REV. VII. 13—17.)

L. M.

LO ! round the throne, at God's right hand,
The saints in countless myriads stand,
Of every tongue redeemed to God,
Arrayed in garments washed in blood.

Through tribulation great they came,
And bore the cross, and scorned the shame :
From all their labours now they rest,
In God's eternal glory blest.

Hunger and thirst they feel no more,
Nor sin, nor pain, nor death deplore ;
The tear is wiped from every eye,
And sorrow yields to endless joy.

They see their Saviour face to face,
And sing the triumphs of His grace :
Him day and night they ceaseless praise,
And thus the loud Hosannas raise :

" Worthy the Lamb, for sinners slain,
" Through endless years to live and reign !
" Thou hast redeemed us by Thy blood,
" And made us kings and priests to God ! "

Mary L. Duncan, ✠ 1840.

(REV. VII. 13—17.)

Eight 7's.

WHO are these in bright array,
  This innumerable throng,
Round the altar, night and day,
  Hymning one triumphant song?
Worthy is the Lamb, once slain,
  Blessing, honour, glory, power,
Might and wisdom to obtain,
  New dominion every hour.

These through fiery trials trod,
  These from great affliction came ;
Now before the throne of God,
  Sealed with His eternal name,
Clad in raiment pure and white,
  Victor palms in every hand,
Through their great Redeemer's might,
  More than conquerors they stand.

Hunger, thirst, disease unknown,
  On immortal fruits they feed ;
Them the Lamb beside the throne
  Shall to living fountains lead :
Joy and gladness banish sighs,
  Perfect love dispels their fears,
And for ever from all eyes
  God shall wipe away all tears.

James Montgomery, 1819.

135

8. 7. 8. 7. 7. 7.

WHO are these, like stars appearing,
　These before God's throne who stand?
Each a golden crown is wearing :
　Who are all this glorious band?
　　Alleluia ! hark, they sing,
　　Praising loud their Heavenly King.

Who are these in dazzling brightness,
　Clothed in God's own righteousness ;
These whose robes of purest whiteness
　Shall their lustre still possess,
　　Still untouch'd by time's rude hand ;—
　　Whence came all this glorious band?

These are they who have contended
　For their Saviour's honour long,
Wrestling on till life was ended,
　Following not the sinful throng :
　　These who well the fight sustained
　　Triumph by the Lamb have gained.

These are they whose hearts were riven,
　Sore with woe and anguish tried,
Who in prayer full oft have striven
　With the God they glorified :
　　Now, their painful conflict o'er,
　　God has bid them weep no more.

Frances E. Cox, 1841,
from the German of H. T. Schenck, ✠ 1727.

136

C. M.

THE Son of God goes forth to war,
  A kingly crown to gain :
His blood-red banner streams afar !
  Who follows in His train ?

Who best can drink His cup of woe,
  Triumphant over pain,
Who patient bears His cross below,
  He follows in His train !

The martyr first whose eagle eye
  Could pierce beyond the grave ;
Who saw his Master in the sky,
  And called on Him to save.

Like Him, with pardon on His tongue,
  In midst of mortal pain,
He prayed for them who did the wrong :
  Who follows in his train ?

A glorious band, the chosen few,
  On whom the Spirit came,
Twelve valiant saints, their hope they knew,
  And mocked the cross and flame.

They climbed the steep ascent of heaven,
  Through peril, toil and pain :
O God, to us may grace be given
  To follow in their train !

Bishop Heber, 1827.

137

O WHAT if we are Christ's,
  Is earthly shame or loss?
Bright shall the crown of glory be,
  When we have borne the cross.

Keen was the trial once,
  Bitter the cup of woe,
When martyred saints, baptized in blood,
  Christ's sufferings shared below.

Bright is their glory now,
  Boundless their joy above,
Where on the bosom of their God,
  They rest in perfect love.

Lord ! may that grace be ours,
  Like them in faith to bear
All that of sorrow, grief, or pain,
  May be our portion here !

Enough, if Thou at last
  The word of blessing give,
And let us rest beneath Thy feet,
  Where saints and angels live !

Sir Henry W. Baker, 1852.

138

C. M.

O JESUS, Lord, the Way, the Truth,
  The Life, the Crown of all
Who here on earth confess Thy name,
  Oh hear us when we call !

We bring to mind with grateful joy,
  Thy servants, who of old
Withstood the snares of earth and hell,
  And now Thy face behold :

Who sought on earth the joys of prayer,
  And that communion knew
Which saints and angels share above
  With holy men and true.

O Lord, Thy Holy Spirit send !
  May grace to us be given
Like them to live and die in Thee,
  And with them rise to heaven.

139

8. 7. 8. 7.

JESUS calls us—o'er the tumult
  Of our life's tempestuous sea
Day by day His sweet voice soundeth,
  Saying, " Christian, follow Me."

Jesus calls us—from the worship
  Of the vain world's golden store,
From each idol that would keep us,
  Saying, " Christian, love Me more."

In our joys and in our sorrows,
  Days of toil and hours of ease,
Still He calls, 'midst cares and pleasures,
  " Christian, love Me more than these."

Jesus calls us—by Thy mercies,
  Saviour ! may we hear Thy call,
Give our hearts to Thy obedience,
  Serve and love Thee best of all.

Cecil F. Alexander, 1858.

D. C. M.

FATHER, before Thy throne of light
  The guardian Angels bend,
And ever in Thy presence bright,
  Their psalms adoring blend ;
And casting down each golden crown
  Beside the crystal sea,
With voice and lyre, in happy quire,
  Hymn glory, Lord, to Thee.

And as the rainbow lustre falls
  Athwart their glowing wings,
While seraph unto seraph calls,
  And each Thy goodness sings ;
So may we feel, as low we kneel,
  To pray Thee for Thy grace,
That Thou art here for all who fear
  The brightness of Thy face.

Here, where the Angels see us come
  To worship day by day,
Teach us to seek our heavenly home,
  And love Thee e'en as they ;
Teach us to raise our notes of praise,
  With them Thy love to own,
That boyhood's time and manhood's prime
  Be Thine and Thine alone.

Frederick W. Farrar, 1856.

141

L. M.

AROUND the throne of God a band
Of bright and glorious angels stand;
Sweet harps within their hands they hold,
And on their heads are crowns of gold.

Some wait around Him, ready still
To sing His praise and do His will;
And some when He commands them, go
To guard His servants here below.

Lord, give Thine angels every day
Command to guard us on our way,
And bid them every evening keep
Their watch around us while we sleep.

So shall no wicked thing draw near
To do us harm or cause us fear,
And we shall dwell, when life is past,
With angels round Thy throne at last.

John M. Neale, 1854.

8. 7. 8. 7.

BRIGHT the vision that delighted
　Once the sight of Judah's seer ;
Sweet the countless tongues united
　To entrance the prophet's ear.

Round the Lord in glory seated,
　Cherubim and Seraphim
Filled His temple, and repeated
　Each to each the alternate hymn :

" Lord, Thy glory fills the heaven :
　Earth is with its fulness stored ;
Unto Thee be glory given,
　Holy, holy, holy, Lord."

Heaven is still with glory ringing,
　Earth takes up the angels' cry,
" Holy, holy, holy," singing.
　" Lord of hosts, Lord God most high."

With His Seraph train before Him,
　With His holy Church below,
Thus unite we to adore Him,
　Bid we thus our anthem flow :

" Lord, Thy glory fills the heaven ;
　Earth is with its fulness stored ;
Unto Thee be glory given,
　Holy, holy, holy, Lord."

Bishop Mant, 1832.

143

Six 8's.

O GOD, with Whom the happy dead
Still live, united to their Head,
 Their Lord and ours alike the same,
For all Thy saints to memory dear,
Departed in Thy faith and fear,
 We bless and praise Thy holy name.

By the same grace upheld, may we
So follow those who followed Thee,
 That with them we may all partake
The free reward of heavenly bliss.
O gracious Father, grant us this,
 For Christ our dear Redeemer's sake !

Josiah Conder, 1837

L

144

D. 7. 6. 7. 6.

THE Church's one foundation
　Is Jesus Christ her Lord ;
She is His new creation
　By water and the word :
From heaven He came and sought her
　To be His holy bride ;
With His own blood He bought her,
　And for her life He died.

Elect from every nation,
　Yet one o'er all the earth,
Her charter of salvation,
　One Lord, one faith, one birth ;
One holy name she blesses,
　Partakes one holy food,
And to one hope she presses
　With every grace endued.

Mid toil and tribulation
　And tumult of her war,
She waits the consummation
　Of peace for evermore ;
Till with the vision glorious
　Her longing eyes are blest,
And the great Church victorious
　Shall be the Church at rest.

Yet she on earth hath union
　With God the Three in One,
And mystic sweet communion
　With those whose rest is won ;
O happy ones and holy !
　Lord, give us grace that we,
Like them the meek and lowly,
　On high may dwell with Thee.

Samuel J. Stone, 1868.

145

C. M.

LET saints on earth in concert sing
 With those whose work is done,
For all the servants of our King
 In earth and heaven are one.

One family we dwell in Him,
 One Church above, beneath,
Though now divided by the stream,
 The narrow stream, of death.

One army of the living God,
 To His command we bow ;
Part of the host have crossed the flood,
 And part are crossing now.

E'en now to their eternal home
 There pass some spirits blest ;
While others to the margin come,
 Waiting their call to rest.

Jesu ! be Thou our constant guide ;
 Then, when the word is given,
Bid death's cold flood its waves divide,
 And give us rest in heaven.

Varied from Charles Wesley, 1759.

146

L. M.

O THOU who makest souls to shine
With light from lighter worlds above,
And droppest glistening dew divine
On all who seek a Saviour's love ;

Do Thou Thy benediction give
On all who teach, on all who learn,
That so Thy Church may holier live,
And every lamp more brightly burn.

Give those who teach pure hearts and wise,
Faith, hope, and love, all warmed by prayer ;
Themselves first training for the skies,
They best will raise their people there.

Give those who learn the willing ear,
The spirit meek, the guileless mind ;
Such gifts will make the lowliest here
Far better than a kingdom find.

O bless the shepherd ; bless the sheep ;
That guide and guided both be one,
One in the faithful watch they keep,
Until this hurrying life be done.

If thus, good Lord, Thy grace be given,
In Thee to live, in Thee to die,
Before we upward pass to heaven
We taste our immortality.

Bishop Armstrong, ✠ 1856.

147

L. M.

LORD, pour Thy Spirit from on high,
And Thine ordainèd servants bless ;
Graces and gifts to each supply,
And clothe Thy priests with righteousness.

Within Thy temple when they stand,
To teach the truth as taught by Thee,
Saviour, like stars in Thy right hand,
Let all Thy Church's pastors be.

Wisdom, and zeal, and love impart,
Firmness and meekness from above,
To bear Thy people in their heart,
And love the souls whom Thou dost love.

To love, and pray, and never faint,
By day and night their guard to keep,
To warn the sinner, form the saint,
To feed Thy lambs and tend Thy sheep.

So, when their work is finished here,
They may in hope their charge resign,
So, when their Master shall appear,
They may with crowns of glory shine.

James Montgomery, 1825.

148

5. 5. 8. 8. 5. 5.

FROM Thy heavenly throne,
Son of God, make known
Now Thy power, Thy Spirit send us,
Strength for this great work to lend us,
That we all may be
Wholly given to Thee.

Thou our hearts prepare,
Shed Thy gladness there,
That we boldly may confess Thee
As our only Lord, and bless Thee,
Whose most precious blood
Flowed to work our good.

Draw our hearts above,
Fill them with Thy love,
So to keep the vows we offer,
Scorning all that earth can proffer,
Truly day by day
Walking in Thy way.

And as we draw near
For Thy blessing here,
May Thy grace in heavenly showers
Quicken all our inner powers,
And Thy light and peace
In our hearts increase.

Let Thy Spirit, Lord,
Promised in Thy word,
Keep us steadfastly in union
With Thy faithful saints' communion,
Till in yon blest place
We behold Thy face.

Catherine Winkworth, 1862,
from the German of Marot, nineteenth century.

149

Six 8's.

LORD, shall Thy children come to Thee?
  A boon of love divine we seek:
Brought to Thine arms in infancy,
  Ere heart could feel or tongue could speak,
Thy children pray for grace, that they
May come themselves to Thee to-day.

Lord, shall we come, and come again
  Oft as we see yon table spread,
And—tokens of Thy dying pain—
  The wine poured out, the broken bread?
Bless, bless, O Lord, Thy children's prayer,
That they may come and find Thee there.

Lord, may we come, not thus alone
  At holy time or solemn rite,
But every hour till life be flown,
  Through weal or woe, in gloom or light;
Still let us seek Thy grace, that we
In faith, hope, love, confirmed may be.

Lord, shall we come—come yet again?
  Thy children ask one blessing more;—
To come, not now alone, but then,
  When life and death and time are o'er:
Then, then to come, O Lord, and be
Confirmed in Heaven, confirmed by Thee.

Bishop Hinds, 1834.

150

Six 7's.

LORD, Thy children guide and keep,
　As with feeble steps they press
On the pathway rough and steep
　Through this weary wilderness.
　　Holy Jesu, day by day
　　Lead us in the narrow way.

There are stony paths to tread ;—
　Give the strength we sorely lack :
There are tangled paths to thread ;—
　Light us, lest we miss the track.
　　Holy Jesu, day by day
　　Lead us in the narrow way.

There are sandy wastes that lie
　Cold and sunless, vast and drear,
Where the feeble faint and die ;—
　Grant us grace to persevere.
　　Holy Jesu, day by day
　　Lead us in the narrow way.

There are soft and flowery glades,
　Decked with golden-fruited trees ;
Sunny slopes, and scented shades ;—
　Keep us, Lord, from slothful ease.
　　Holy Jesu, day by day
　　Lead us in the narrow way.

Upward still to purer heights,
　Onward yet to scenes more blest,
Calmer regions, clearer lights,
　Till we reach the promised rest.
　　Holy Jesu, day by day
　　Lead us in the narrow way.

William W. How, 1860.

151

Four 7's.

THINE for ever! God of love,
Hear us from Thy throne above:
Thine for ever may we be,
Here and in eternity.

Thine for ever! Lord of life,
Shield us through our earthly strife;
Thou the Life, the Truth, the Way,
Guide us to the realms of day.

Thine for ever! Oh, how blest,
They who find in Thee their rest!
Saviour, Guardian, heavenly Friend,
Oh, defend us to the end!

Thine for ever! Saviour, keep
Us Thy frail and trembling sheep;
Safe alone beneath Thy care,
Let us all Thy goodness share.

Thine for ever! Thou our Guide,
All our wants by Thee supplied,
All our sins by Thee forgiven,
Lead us, Lord, from earth to heaven.

Mary F. Maude, 1848.

152

C. M.

IN token that thou shalt not fear
   Christ crucified to own,
We print the cross upon thee here,
   And stamp thee His alone.

In token that thou shalt not blush
   To glory in His name,
We blazon here upon thy front
   His glory and His shame.

In token that thou shalt not flinch
   Christ's quarrel to maintain,
But 'neath His banner manfully
   Firm at thy post remain.

In token that thou too shalt tread
   The path He travelled by,
Endure the cross, despise the shame,
   And sit thee down on high.

Thus outwardly and visibly
   We seal thee for His own ;
And may the brow that wears His cross
   Hereafter share His crown !

Henry Alford, 1832.

153

(EPH. VI. 11—18.)

S. M.

SOLDIERS of Christ, arise
And put your armour on,
Strong in the strength which God supplies
Through His Eternal Son.

Strong in the Lord of Hosts,
And in His mighty power ;
Who in the strength of Jesus trusts
Is more than conqueror.

Stand, then, in His great might,
With all His strength endowed :
But take, to arm you for the fight,
The panoply of God ;

That, having all things done,
And all your conflicts past,
Ye may o'ercome, through Christ alone,
And stand complete at last.

Charles Wesley, 1749.

154

L. M.

MY God, and is Thy table spread ;
   And does Thy cup with love o'erflow ?
Thither be all Thy children led,
   And let them all its sweetness know.

Hail, sacred feast, which Jesus makes !
   Rich banquet of His flesh and blood.
Thrice happy he, who here partakes
   That sacred stream, that heavenly food !

Oh, let Thy table honoured be,
   And furnished well with joyful guests ;
And may each soul salvation see
   That here its sacred pledges tastes.

Revive Thy dying churches, Lord !
   And bid our drooping graces live ;
And more, that energy afford
   A Saviour's love alone can give !

Philip Doddridge, 1755.

155

Four 7's.

BREAD of Heaven ! on Thee we feed ;
For Thy flesh is meat indeed :
Ever let our souls be fed
With this true and living Bread.

Rock of Heaven ! Thy vital stream
Drink indeed may we esteem !
He to whom those waters flow
Thirst and drought no more shall know.

Lamb of God ! we lift our eyes
To Thy perfect sacrifice :
Lord, Thy wounds our healing give ;
To Thy cross we look and live.

Day by day with strength supplied
Through the life of Him who died,
May our daily drink and food
Be Thy body and Thy blood.

Altered from Josiah Conder, 1824.

156

Eight 8's.

LORD, to Thine altar we draw near ;
Oh, fence us round with holy fear,
And o'er our trembling spirits shed
The feeling of Thy presence dread.
We bow the head, we bend the knee,
Before Thine awful majesty,
Beseeching Thee with favouring eyes
To look upon our sacrifice.

Our conflict, Lord, Thou know'st it all,
The thousand foes that fast enthral
Our captive souls, that would be free
From every taint, to worship Thee ;
The vain desire, the wandering thought,
With worldliness and folly fraught,
The earthly joy, the earthly care,
That haunt us in Thy house of prayer.

The world, the flesh, and Satan's rage,
Our threefold foe, Thou canst assuage ;
Thou, who by Thine almighty power
Didst quell them in their fiercest hour !
Oh, let Thy new and risen life
Within our souls subdue the strife ;
And help us, Lord, that we may see
Thy presence here, and worship Thee.

Sarah Farmer, 1842.

157

P. M.

DECK thyself, my soul, with gladness,
Leave the gloomy haunts of sadness,
Come into the daylight's splendour,
There with joy thy praises tender
Unto Him whose grace unbounded
Hath this wondrous banquet founded :
High o'er all the heavens He reigneth,
Yet to dwell with thee He deigneth.

Sun, who all my life doth brighten,
Light, who dost my soul enlighten,
Joy, the sweetest man e'er knoweth,
Fount, whence all my being floweth,
At Thy feet I cry, my Maker,
Let me be a fit partaker
Of this blessèd food from heaven,
For our good, Thy glory, given.

Jesus, Bread of life, I pray Thee,
Let me gladly here obey Thee ;
Never to my hurt invited,
Be Thy love with love requited ;
From this banquet let me measure,
Lord, how vast and deep its treasure ;
Through the gifts Thou here dost give me
As Thy guest in heaven receive me.

Catherine Winkworth, 1858,
from the German of J. Frank, 1653.

158

C. M.

ACCORDING to Thy gracious word,
  In meek humility,
This will I do, my dying Lord,
  I will remember Thee.

Thy body, broken for my sake,
  My bread from heaven shall be ;
Thy testamental cup I take,
  And thus remember Thee.

When to the cross I turn mine eyes,
  And rest on Calvary,
O Lamb of God, my sacrifice,
  I must remember Thee :—

Remember Thee, and all Thy pains,
  And all Thy love to me ;
Yea, while a breath, a pulse remains,
  Will I remember Thee.

And when these failing lips grow dumb,
  And mind and memory flee,
When Thou shalt in Thy kingdom come,
  Jesus, remember me.

James Montgomery, 1819.

159

Six 10's.

AND now, O Father, mindful of the love
  That bought us once for all on Calvary's tree,
And having with us Him that pleads above,
  We here present, we here spread forth to Thee
That only Offering perfect in Thine eyes,
The one true, pure, immortal Sacrifice.

Look, Father, look on His anointed face,
  And only look on us as found in Him ;
Look not on our misusings of Thy grace,
  Our prayer so languid, and our faith so dim ;
For lo ! between our sins and their reward
We set the passion of Thy Son, our Lord.

And then for those, our dearest and our best,
  By this prevailing Presence we appeal ;
Oh, fold them closer to Thy mercy's breast,
  Oh, do Thine utmost for their soul's true weal ;
From tainting mischief keep them white and clear,
And crown Thy gifts with strength to persevere.

And so we come ; Oh, draw us to Thy feet,
  Most patient Saviour, who canst love us still ;
And by this food, so awful and so sweet,
  Deliver us from every touch of ill :
In Thine own service make us glad and free,
And grant us never more to part with Thee.

William Bright, 1875.

160

Six 8's.

FORGIVE, O Lord, our wanderings past,
  Henceforth we would obey Thy call ;
Our sins far from us may we cast,
  And turn to Thee devoutly all :
Then with archangels we shall sing
High praise to Heaven's Eternal King.

Hear us, O Lord, in mercy hear ;
  With sorrow we our guilt deplore :
Pity our grief, and calm our fear,
  And give us grace to sin no more :
Then with archangels we shall sing
High praise to Heaven's Eternal King.

While at Thy table, Lord, we kneel,
  And of Thy holy feast partake ;
Our pardon there vouchsafe to seal,
  For Jesus our Redeemer's sake :
Then with archangels we shall sing
High praise to Heaven's Eternal King.

J. Kempthorne, 1809.

161

C. M.

O GOD, unseen, yet ever near,
  Thy presence may we feel ;
And thus inspired with holy fear,
  Before Thine altar kneel.

Here may Thy faithful people know
  The blessings of Thy love ;
The streams that through the desert flow,
  The manna from above.

We come obedient to Thy word,
  To feast on heavenly food :
Our meat the Body of the Lord ;
  Our drink, His precious Blood.

Thus would we all Thy words obey ;
  For we, O God, are Thine ;
And go rejoicing on our way,
  Renewed with strength divine !

Edward Osler, 1837.

162

L. M.

JESUS, Thou Joy of loving hearts !
  Thou Fount of life ! Thou Light of men !
From the best bliss that earth imparts,
  We turn unfilled to Thee again.

Thy truth unchanged hath ever stood :
  Thou savest those that on Thee call ;
To them that seek Thee, Thou art good,
  To them that find Thee, All in all.

We taste Thee, O Thou living Bread,
  And long to feast upon Thee still ;
We drink of Thee, the Fountain-head,
  And thirst our souls from Thee to fill.

Our restless spirits yearn for Thee,
  Where'er our changeful lot is cast ;
Glad when Thy gracious smile we see,
  Blest when our faith can hold Thee fast.

O Jesus, ever with us stay !
  Make all our moments calm and bright ;
Chase the dark night of sin away,
  Shed o'er the world Thy holy light.

Ray Palmer, 1833,
from the Latin of St. Bernard, ✠ 1153.

163

Four 10's.

THEE we adore, O hidden Saviour, Thee,
Who in Thy feast with us vouchsaf'st to be ;
Both flesh and spirit at Thy presence fail,
Yet here Thy presence we devoutly hail.

O blest memorial of our dying Lord,
Who living bread to men dost here afford !
Oh, may our souls for ever feed on Thee,
And Thou, O Chirst, for ever precious be !

Fountain of goodness ! Jesu, Lord and God !
Cleanse us, unclean, with Thy most cleansing Blood :
Increase our faith and love, that we may know
The hope and peace which from Thy presence flow.

O Christ ! Whom now beneath a veil we see,
May what we thirst for soon our portion be—
To gaze on Thee unveiled, and see Thy face,
The vision of Thy glory and Thy grace.

Bishop Woodford, 1863,
from the Latin of St. Thomas Aquinas, ✠ 1274.

164

THOU art gone to the grave! but we will not
  deplore thee ;
Though sorrows and darkness encompass the tomb,
The Saviour has passed through its portal before
  thee,
And the lamp of His love is thy guide through the
  gloom.

Thou art gone to the grave ! we no longer behold
  thee,
Nor tread the rough path of the world by thy side ;
But the wide arms of Mercy are spread to enfold thee,
And sinners may die, for the Sinless has died !

Thou art gone to the grave ! and, its mansion for-
  saking,
Perchance thy weak spirit in fear lingered long ;
But the mild rays of Paradise beamed on thy waking,
And the sound which thou heard'st was the Sera-
  phim's song.

Thou art gone to the grave ! but we will not deplore
  thee,
Whose God was thy Ramsom, thy Guardian and
  Guide :
He gave thee, He took thee, and He will restore thee,
And death hath no sting, for the Saviour has died.

Bishop Heber, 1827.

165

7. 7. 7. 7. 8. 8.

NOW the labourer's task is o'er ;
  Now the battle-day is past ;
Now upon the farther shore
  Lands the voyager at last.
Father, in Thy gracious keeping
Leave we now Thy servant sleeping.

There the tears of earth are dried ;
  There its hidden things are clear :
There the work of life is tried
  By a juster Judge than here.
Father, in Thy gracious keeping
Leave we now Thy servant sleeping.

There the sinful souls, that turn
  To the Cross their dying eyes,
All the love of Christ shall learn
  At His feet in Paradise.
Father, in Thy gracious keeping
Leave we now Thy servant sleeping.

There no more the powers of hell
  Can prevail to mar their peace ;
Christ the Lord shall guard them well,
  He who died for their release.
Father, in Thy gracious keeping
Leave we now Thy servant sleeping.

" Earth to earth and dust to dust,"
  Calmly now the words we say,
Leaving him to sleep in trust
  Till the Resurrection day.
Father, in Thy gracious keeping
Leave we now Thy servant sleeping.

John Ellerton, 1875.

166

FROM Greenland's icy mountains,
   From India's coral strand,
Where Afric's sunny fountains
   Roll down their golden sand ;
From many an ancient river,
   From many a palmy plain,
They call us to deliver
   Their land from error's chain.

What though the spicy breezes
   Blow soft o'er Ceylon's isle,
Though every prospect pleases,
   And only man is vile ;
In vain with lavish kindness
   The gifts of God are strown ;
The heathen in his blindness
   Bows down to wood and stone !

Can we whose souls are lighted
   With wisdom from on high,
Can we to men benighted
   The lamp of life deny ?
Salvation ! O Salvation !
   The joyful sound proclaim,
Till each remotest nation
   Has learned Messiah's Name !

Waft, waft, ye winds, His story,
   And you, ye waters, roll,
Till, like a sea of glory,
   It spreads from pole to pole !
Till o'er our ransomed nature
   The Lamb for sinners slain,
Redeemer, King, Creator,
   In bliss returns to reign !

Bishop Heber, 1819.

167

6. 6. 4. 6. 6. 6. 4.

THOU, whose Almighty word
Chaos and darkness heard
　And took their flight ;
Hear us we humbly pray ;
And, where the Gospel's day
Sheds not its glorious ray,
　Let there be light !

Thou, who didst come to bring
On Thy redeeming wing
　Healing and sight,
Health to the sick in mind,
Sight to the inly blind,
Oh, now to all mankind
　Let there be light !

Spirit of truth and love,
Life-giving, holy Dove,
　Speed forth Thy flight !
Move on the water's face,
Bearing the lamp of grace,
And in earth's darkest place
　Let there be light !

Holy and blessed Three,
Glorious Trinity,
　Wisdom, Love, Might !
Boundless as ocean's tide
Rolling in fullest pride,
Through the earth, far and wide
　Let there be light !

John Marriott, 1813.

168

8. 7. 8. 7. 4. 7.

SOULS in heathen darkness lying,
  Where no light has broken through -
Souls that Jesus bought by dying,
  Whom His soul in travail knew—
      Thousand voices,
  Call us o'er the waters blue.

Christians, hearken ! none has taught them
  Of His love so deep and dear ;
Of the precious price that bought them.
  Of the nail, the thorn, the spear ;
      Ye who know Him,
  Guide them from their darkness drear.

Haste, O haste, and spread the tidings
  Wide to earth's remotest strand ;
Let no brother's bitter chidings
  Rise against us, when we stand
      In the judgment,
  From some far, forgotten land.

Lo ! the hills for harvest whiten
  All along each distant shore ;
Seaward far the islands brighten—
  Light of nations ! lead us o'er :
      When we seek them,
  Let Thy Spirit go before.

                    Cecil F. Alexander, 1850.

169

Eight 7's.

HARK ! the song of jubilee,
   Loud as mighty thunder's roar,
Or the fulness of the sea
   When it breaks upon the shore :
Alleluia ! for the Lord
   God Omnipotent shall reign ;
Alleluia ! let the word
   Echo round the earth and main.

Alleluia ! hark, the sound
   From the centre to the skies
Wakes above, beneath, around,
   All creation's harmonies !
See Jehovah's banners furled,
   Sheathed His sword : He speaks, 'tis done ;
And the kingdoms of this world
   Are the kingdoms of His Son.

He shall reign from pole to pole,
   With illimitable sway ;
He shall reign, when like a scroll
   Yonder heavens have past away.
Then the end :— beneath His rod
   Man's last enemy shall fall :
Alleluia ! Christ in God,
   God in Christ, is all in all.

James Montgomery, 1819.

170

(Isaiah LII. 7—10.)

S. M.

HOW beauteous are their feet,
Who stand on Sion's hill ;
Who bring salvation on their tongues,
And words of peace instil !

How happy are our ears,
That hear the joyful sound,
Which kings and prophets waited for,
And sought, but never found !

How blessèd are our eyes,
That see this heavenly light ;
Prophets and kings desired it long,
But died without the sight !

O Lord, send forth Thy truth,
Make known Thy name abroad ;
Till all the nations shall behold
Their Saviour and their God.

Isaac Watts, 1709.

171

(PSALM LXVII.)

TO bless Thy chosen race,
In mercy, Lord, incline ;
And cause the brightness of Thy face
On all Thy saints to shine.

That so Thy wondrous way
May through the world be known ;
While distant lands their tribute pay,
And Thy salvation own.

Let diff'ring nations join
To celebrate Thy fame ;
Let all the world, O Lord, combine
To praise Thy glorious name.

O let them shout and sing
With joy and pious mirth :
For Thou, the righteous Judge and King,
Shalt govern all the earth.

Then God upon our land
Shall constant blessings shower ;
And all the world in awe shall stand
Of His resistless power.

Tate and Brady, 1696.

172

8. 8. 8. 4.

O LORD of heaven, and earth, and sea,
To Thee all praise and glory be ;
How shall we shew our love to Thee,
    Who givest all ?

The golden sunshine, vernal air,
Sweet flowers and fruit, Thy love declare ;
When harvests ripen, Thou art there,
    Who givest all.

For peaceful homes, and healthful days,
For all the blessings earth displays,
We owe Thee thankfulness and praise,
    Who givest all.

For souls redeemed, for sins forgiven,
For means of grace and hopes of heaven,
Father, what can to Thee be given,
    Who givest all ?

We lose what on ourselves we spend,
We have as treasure without end
Whatever, Lord, to Thee we lend,
    Who givest all.

Whatever, Lord, we lend to Thee,
Repaid a thousandfold will be ;
Then gladly will we give to Thee,
    Who givest all.

To Thee, from whom we all derive
Our life, our gifts, our power to give ;
Oh, may we ever with Thee live,
    Who givest all.

Bishop Chr. Wordsworth, 1865.

173   D. 7.6.7.6—6.6.8.4.

WE plough the fields and scatter
   The good seed on the land,
But it is fed and watered
   By God's almighty hand ;
He sends the snow in winter,
   The warmth to swell the grain,
The breezes, and the sunshine,
   And soft refreshing rain.
     All good gifts around us
     Are sent from heaven above,
Then thank the Lord, O thank the Lord,
     For all His love.

He only is the maker
   Of all things near and far :
He paints the wayside flower,
   He lights the evening star ;
The winds and waves obey Him,
   By Him the birds are fed :
Much more to us, His children,
   He gives our daily bread.
     All good gifts around us, &c.

We thank Thee, then, O Father,
   For all things bright and good,
The seed-time and the harvest,
   Our life, our health, our food ;
Accept the gifts we offer
   For all Thy love imparts,
And, what Thou most desirest,
   Our humble, thankful hearts.
     All good gifts around us
     Are sent from heaven above,
Then thank the Lord, O thank the Lord,
     For all His love.

Charles S. Bere,
from the German of Matthias Claudius, 1783.

174

Six 8's.

LORD of the harvest, once again
We thank Thee for the ripened grain ;
For crops safe carried, sent to cheer
Thy servants through another year ;
For all sweet holy thoughts supplied
By seed-time and by harvest-tide.

The bare dead grain, in Autumn sown,
Its robe of vernal green puts on ;
Glad from its wintry grave it springs,
Fresh garnished by the King of kings :
So, Lord, to those who sleep in Thee,
Shall new and glorious bodies be.

Nor vainly of Thy word we ask
A lesson from the reaper's task :
So shall Thine angels issue forth ;
The tares be burnt ; the just of earth,
To wind and storm exposed no more,
Be gathered to their Father's store.

Daily, O Lord, our prayers be said,
As Thou hast taught, for daily bread ;
But not alone our bodies feed,
Supply our fainting spirits' need :
O Bread of life, from day to day,
Be Thou their comfort, food, and stay.

Joseph Anstice, 1836.

175

C. M.

LORD, in Thy Name Thy servants plead,
  And Thou hast sworn to hear :
Thine is the harvest, Thine the seed,
  The fresh and fading year.

Our hope, when autumn winds blew wild,
  We trusted, Lord, with Thee ;
And now that spring has on us smiled,
  We wait on Thy decree.

The former and the latter rain,
  The summer sun and air,
The green ear. and the golden grain,
  All Thine, are ours by prayer.

Thine too by right, and ours by grace,
  The wondrous growth unseen,
The hopes that soothe, the fears that brace,
  The love that shines serene !

So grant the precious things brought forth
  By sun and moon below,
That Thee, in Thy new heaven and earth,
  We never may forego.

John Keble, 1857.

N

176

Six 8's.

ETERNAL Father, strong to save,
Whose arm hath bound the restless wave,
Who bidd'st the mighty ocean deep
Its own appointed limits keep ;
   O hear us when we cry to Thee
   For those in peril on the sea.

O Christ, whose voice the waters heard
And hushed their raging at Thy word,
Who walkedst on the foaming deep,
And calm amid the storm didst sleep ;
   O hear us when we cry to Thee
   For those in peril on the sea.

O Holy Spirit, who didst brood
Upon the waters dark and rude,
And bid their angry tumult cease,
And give, for wild confusion, peace ;
   O hear us when we cry to Thee
   For those in peril on the sea.

O Trinity of love and power,
Our brethren shield in danger's hour ;
From rock and tempest, fire and foe,
Protect them wheresoe'er they go ;
   Thus evermore shall rise to Thee
   Glad hymns of praise from land and sea.

William Whiting, 1860.
(*Varied by compilers of Hymns A. and M.,* 1861.)

177

L. M.

FATHER, hear Thy children's praises
  For the boon we own to-day ;
Grateful love our hearts upraises,
  This our sacrifice to pay :

Thanks for all Thy mercies given,
  Stores of knowledge here unrolled,
Means of grace and hopes of heaven,
  Unto us, Thy chosen fold !

Lord, Thy servants' spirits turning,
  Mould them by Thy gracious sway :
Godliness and all good learning
  May we follow, day by day !

May we, these Thy bounties sharing,
  Every talent use aright,
Still by earthly lore preparing,
  Till our faith be turned to sight :

Till, undimmed by dark reflection,
  Face to face shall Christ be shown ;
Knowledge rise to full perfection—
  Knowing e'en as we are known.

Henry J. Buckoll, ✠ 1871.

N 2

178

8. 7. 8. 7. 4. 7.

LORD, behold us with Thy blessing,
  Once again assembled here ;
Onward be our footsteps pressing,
  In Thy love, and faith, and fear :
    Still protect us
  By Thy presence ever near !

For Thy mercy we adore Thee,
  For this rest upon our way ;
Lord, again we bow before Thee,
  Speed our labours day by day :
    Mind and spirit
  With Thy choicest gifts array !

Keep the spell of home affection
  Still alive in every heart ;
May its power, with mild direction,
  Draw our love from self apart,
    Till Thy children
  Feel that Thou their Father art !

Break temptation's fatal power,
  Shielding all with guardian care,
Safe in every careless hour,
  Safe from sloth and sensual snare :
    Thou, our Saviour,
  Still our failing strength repair !

Henry J. Buckoll, ✠ 187 ..

8. 7. 8. 7. 4. 7.

LORD, dismiss us with Thy blessing ;
  Thanks for mercies past receive ;
Pardon all, their faults confessing ;
  Time that's lost may all retrieve !
    May Thy children
  Ne'er again Thy Spirit grieve !

Bless Thou all our days of leisure ;
  Help us selfish lures to flee ;
Sanctify our every pleasure,
  Pure and blameless may it be :
    May our gladness
  Draw us evermore to Thee !

By Thy kindly influence cherish
  All the good we here have gained ;
May all taint of evil perish,
  By Thy mightier power restrained ;
    Seek we ever
  Knowledge pure and love unfeigned !

Let Thy father-hand be shielding
  All who here shall meet no more ;
May their seed-time past be yielding
  Year by year a richer store !
    Those returning
  Make more faithful than before !

Henry J. Buckoll, ✠ 1871.

180

P. M.

WHEN the Lord recalls the banished,
  Frees the captives all at last,
Every sorrow will have vanished,
  Like a dream when night is past:
Then shall all our hearts rejoice,
And with glad resounding voice
We shall praise the Lord who sought us,
For the freedom He hath wrought us.

Lift Thy hand to aid us, Father,
  Look on us who widely roam,
And Thy scattered children gather
  In their longed-for promised home :
Steep and weary is the way,
Shorten Thou the sultry day,
Faithful warriors hast Thou found us,
Let Thy peace for aye surround us.

In that peace we reap in gladness
  What was sown in tearful showers ;
There the fruit of all our sadness
  Ripens —there the palm is ours ;
There our God upon His throne
Is our full reward alone ;
They who all for God surrender
Bring their sheaves in heavenly splendour.

Catherine Winkworth, 1858,
from the German of S. G. Bürde, 1794.

181

Six 8's.

I PRAISED the earth, in beauty seen,
With garlands gay of various green ;
I praised the sea, whose ample field
Shone glorious as a silver shield ;
And earth and ocean seemed to say,
" Our beauties are but for a day."

I praised the sun, whose chariot rolled
On wheels of amber and of gold ;
I praised the moon, whose softer eye
Gleamed sweetly through the summer sky ;
And moon and sun in answer said,
" Our days of light are numberèd."

O God, O Good beyond compare !
If thus Thy meaner works are fair,
If thus Thy bounties gild the span
Of ruined earth and sinful man,
How glorious must the mansion be,
Where Thy redeemed shall dwell with Thee !

Bishop Heber, 1827.

182

L. M.

YES, God is good ; in earth and sky,
　From ocean depths and spreading wood,
Ten thousand voices seem to cry,
　" God made us all, and God is good."

The sun that keeps his trackless way,
　And downward pours his golden flood,
Night's sparkling hosts, all seem to say
　In accents clear, that God is good.

The merry birds prolong the strain,
　Their song with every spring renewed :
And balmy air, and falling rain,
　Each softly whisper, " God is good."

I hear it in the rushing breeze ;
　The hills that have for ages stood,
The echoing sky and roaring seas,
　All swell the chorus, " God is good."

Yes, God is good, all nature says,
　By God's own hand with speech endued ;
And man, in louder notes of praise,
　Should sing for joy that God is good.

For all Thy gifts we bless Thee, Lord ;
　But chiefly for our heavenly food,
Thy pardoning grace, Thy quickening word :
　These prompt our song that God is good.

John H. Gurney, 1851.

183

L. M.

LO, heaven and earth, and sea and air,
Their Maker's glory all declare ;
And thou, my soul, awake and sing,
To Him thy praises also bring.

Through Him the glorious source of day
Drives all the clouds of night away ;
The pomp of stars, the moon's soft light,
Praise Him through all the silent night.

Behold, how He hath everywhere
Made earth so wondrous rich and fair ;
The forest dark, the fruitful land,
All living things do show His hand.

My God, how wondrously dost Thou
Unfold Thyself to us e'en now !
O grave it deeply on my heart
What I am, Lord, and what Thou art !

Catherine Winkworth, 1858,
from the German of Joachim Neander, 1679.

184

L. M.

WE thank Thee, Lord, for this fair earth,
  The glittering sky, the silver sea,
For all their beauty, all their worth,
  Their light and glory, come from Thee.

Thanks for the flowers that clothe the ground,
  The trees that wave their arms above,
The hills that gird our dwellings round,
  As Thou dost gird Thine own with love.

Yet teach us still how far more fair,
  More glorious, Father, in Thy sight.
Is one pure deed, one holy prayer,
  One heart that owns Thy Spirit's might.

So while we gaze, with thoughtful eye,
  On all the gifts Thy love has given,
Help us in Thee to live and die,
  By Thee to rise from earth to heaven.

Bishop Cotton, ✠ 1866.

185

D. 8. 8. 6.

GO forth, my heart, and seek delight
In all the gifts of God's great might,
  These pleasant summer hours :
Look how the plains for thee and me
Have decked themselves most fair to see,
  All bright and sweet with flowers.

Thy mighty working, mighty God,
Wakes all my powers ; I look abroad,
  And can no longer rest :
I too must sing when all things sing,
And from my heart the praises ring
  The Highest loveth best.

But help me ; let Thy heavenly showers
Revive and bless my fainting powers,
  And let me thrive and grow
Beneath the summer of Thy grace,
And fruits of faith bud forth apace
  While yet I dwell below.

Catherine Winkworth, 1855,
from the German of Paul Gerhardt, 1659.

186

D. 8. 7. 8. 7.

LORD, we thank Thee for the pleasure
  That our happy lifetime gives,
The inestimable treasure
  Of a soul that ever lives ;
Mind that looks before and after,
  Yearning for its home above,
Human tears, and human laughter,
  And the depth of human love ;

For the thrill, the leap, the gladness
  Of our pulses flowing free :
E'en for every touch of sadness
  That may bring us nearer Thee ;
But above all other kindness,
  Thine unutterable love,
Which, to heal our sin and blindness,
  Sent Thy dear Son from above.

Teach us so our days to number,
  That we may be early wise ;
Dreamy mist, or cloud of slumber,
  Never dull our heavenward eyes ;
Hearty be our work, and willing,
  As to Thee, and not to men,
For we know our soul's fulfilling
  Is in heaven ;—not till then.

Thomas W. Jex-Blake, 1855.

187

(PSALM XIX.) Eight 8's.

THE spacious firmament on high,
With all the blue ethereal sky
And spangled heavens, a shining frame,
Their great Original proclaim.
The unwearied sun, from day to day,
Does his Creator's power display,
And publishes to every land
The works of an Almighty hand.

Soon as the evening shades prevail,
The moon takes up the wondrous tale,
And nightly to the listening earth
Repeats the story of her birth ;
Whilst all the stars that round her burn,
And all the planets in their turn,
Confirm the tidings as they roll,
And spread the truth from pole to pole.

What though in solemn silence all
Move round the dark terrestrial ball?
What though no real voice or sound
Amidst their radiant orbs be found ?
In reason's ear they all rejoice,
And utter forth a glorious voice,
For ever singing as they shine,
" The hand that made us is Divine."

Joseph Addison, 1712.

188

(PSALM XXXIV.)

C. M.

THROUGH all the changing scenes of life,
  In trouble and in joy,
The praises of my God shall still
  My heart and tongue employ.

Of His deliverance I will boast,
  Till all that are distrest
From my example comfort take
  And charm their griefs to rest.

The hosts of God encamp around
  The dwellings of the just ;
Deliverance He affords to all
  Who on His succour trust.

Fear Him, ye saints, and you will then
  Have nothing else to fear ;
Make you His service your delight,
  Your wants shall be His care.

To God the Father, God the Son,
  And God the Holy Ghost,
All glory be from saints on earth
  And from the Angel-host.

Tate and Brady, 1696.

189

(PSALM LXVII.)

Six 7's.

GOD of mercy, God of grace,
Show the brightness of Thy face :
Shine upon us, Saviour, shine,
Fill Thy Church with light divine ;
And Thy saving health extend
Unto earth's remotest end.

Let Thy people praise Thee, Lord,
Be by all that live adored :
Let the nations shout and sing
Glory to their Saviour King ;
At Thy feet their tribute pay,
And Thy holy will obey.

Let the people praise Thee, Lord ;
Earth shall then her fruits afford ;
God to man His blessing give,
Man to God devoted live ;
All below, and all above,
One in joy, and light, and love.

Henry F. Lyte, 1847.

190

(Psalm LXXXIV.)

6. 6. 6. 6. 4. 4. 4. 4.

LORD of the worlds above,
How pleasant and how fair,
The dwellings of Thy love,
Thy earthly temples, are !
  To Thine abode
    My heart aspires
    With warm desires
  To see my God.

O happy souls that pray
Where God appoints to hear !
O happy men that pay
Their constant service there !
  They praise Thee still :
    And happy they
    That love the way
  To Sion's hill.

They go from strength to strength.
Through this dark vale of tears,
Till each arrives at length,
Till each in Heaven appears :
  O glorious seat,
    When God our King
    Shall thither bring
  Our willing feet !

Isaac Watts, 1719.

191

(Psalm XCV.)

L. M.

O COME, loud anthems let us sing,
Loud thanks to our almighty King ;
For we our voices high should raise
When our Salvation's Rock we praise.

Into His presence let us haste,
To thank Him for His favours past ;
To Him address in joyful songs
The praise that to His name belongs.

The depths of earth are in His hand,
Her secret wealth at His command ;
The strength of hills that reach the skies
Subjected to His empire lies.

The rolling ocean's vast abyss
By the same sovereign right is His ;
'Tis moved by His almighty hand,
That formed and fixed the solid land.

O let us to His courts repair,
And bow with adoration there ;
Down on our knees devoutly all
Before the Lord our Maker fall.

Tate and Brady, 1696.

192

(Psalm C.)

L. M.

ALL people that on earth do dwell,
   Sing to the Lord with cheerful voice ;
Him serve with fear, His praise forth tell :
   Come ye before Him and rejoice.

The Lord, ye know, is God indeed ;
   Without our aid He did us make ;
We are His flock, He doth us feed,
   And for His sheep He doth us take.

O enter then His gates with praise ;
   Approach with joy His courts unto ;
Praise, laud, and bless His name always,
   For it is seemly so to do.

For why ? the Lord our God is good,
   His mercy is for ever sure ;
His truth at all times firmly stood,
   And shall from age to age endure.

William Kethe, 1561.

193

(Psalm C.)

L. M.

BEFORE Jehovah's awful throne,
  Ye nations, bow with sacred joy ;
Know that the Lord is God alone,
  He can create, and He destroy.

His sovereign power without our aid
  Made us of clay, and formed us men ;
And when like wandering sheep we strayed,
  He brought us to His fold again.

We'll crowd Thy gates with thankful songs,
  High as the heavens our voices raise ;
And earth with her ten thousand tongues
  Shall fill Thy courts with sounding praise.

Wide as the world is Thy command,
  Vast as eternity Thy love ;
Firm as a rock Thy truth shall stand,
  When rolling years shall cease to move.

Varied by Charles Wesley, 1741,
from Isaac Watts, 1719.

194

(Psalm CIV.)

P. M.

O WORSHIP the King all-glorious above ;
O gratefully sing His power and His love ;
Our Shield and Defender, the Ancient of days,
Pavilioned in splendour, and girded with praise.

O tell of His might, O sing of His grace,
Whose robe is the light, whose canopy space ;
His chariots of wrath the deep thunder-clouds form,
And dark is His path on the wings of the storm.

Frail children of dust, and feeble as frail,
In Thee do we trust, nor find Thee to fail.
Thy mercies how tender ! how firm to the end !
Our Maker, Defender, Redeemer, and Friend.

O measureless Might, ineffable Love,
While angels delight to hymn Thee above,
Thy ransomed creation, though feeble their lays,
With true adoration shall sing to Thy praise.

Sir Robert Grant, ✠ 1838
(based on William Kethe's version).

195

(PSALM CXVII.)

L. M.

FROM all who dwell below the skies
Let the Creator's praise arise ;
Let the Redeemer's Name be sung
Through every land, by every tongue !

Eternal are Thy mercies, Lord,
Eternal truth attends Thy word ;
Thy praise shall sound from shore to shore
Till suns shall rise and set no more.

Praise God, from whom all blessings flow ;
Praise Him, all creatures here below ;
Praise Him above, ye heavenly host ;
Praise Father, Son, and Holy Ghost !

Isaac Watts, 1719.

196

D. 8. 7 8. 7.

GOD and Father, great and holy,
　Fearing nought we come to Thee ;
Fearing nought, though weak and lowly,
　For Thy love hath made us free ;
By the blue sky bending o'er us,
　By the green earth's flowery zone,
Teach us, Lord, the angel chorus,
　Thou art love, and love alone !

Father, Lord of all creation,
　Holy, blest, eternal Son,
Spirit, source of inspiration,
　Awful Godhead, Three in One ;
With the notes which, high ascending,
　Ring around the sapphire throne,
May Thy sons the song be blending,
　Thou art love, and love alone !

Though the world in flames should perish,
　Suns and stars in ruin fall,
Trust in Thee our hearts would cherish,
　Thou to us be all in all ;
Yea ! though heavens Thy name are praising,
　Seraphs hymn no sweeter tone
Than the song our hearts are raising,
　Thou art love, and love alone !

Frederic W. Farrar, 1860.

197

(PSALM CXLVIII.)

6. 6. 6. 6. 4. 4. 4. 4.

YE boundless realms of joy,
　Exalt your Maker's fame,
His praise your song employ
　Above the starry frame ;
　　Your voices raise,
　　　Ye cherubim
　　　And seraphim,
　　To sing His praise.

Thou moon that rul'st the night,
　And sun that guid'st the day,
Ye glittering stars of light,
　To Him your homage pay :
　　His praise declare,
　　　Ye heavens above,
　　　And clouds that move
　　In liquid air.

His chosen saints to grace,
　He sets them up on high,
And favours Israel's race,
　Who still to Him are nigh.
　　O therefore raise
　　　Your grateful voice,
　　　And still rejoice
　　The Lord to praise.

Tate and Brady, 1696.

198

C. M.

WHEN all Thy mercies, O my God,
  My rising soul surveys,
Transported with the view, I'm lost
  In wonder, love, and praise.

Unnumbered comforts to my soul
  Thy tender care bestowed,
Before my infant heart conceived
  From whom these comforts flowed.

When worn with sickness, oft hast Thou
  With health renewed my face ;
And, when in sins and sorrows sunk,
  Revived my soul with grace.

Ten thousand thousand precious gifts
  My daily thanks employ ;
Nor is the least a cheerful heart,
  That tastes these gifts with joy.

Through every period of my life
  Thy goodness I'll pursue ;
And after death in distant worlds
  The glorious theme renew.

Through all eternity to Thee
  A joyful song I'll raise ;
For O ! eternity's too short
  To utter all Thy praise.

Joseph Addison, 1712.

199

C. M.

HOW sweet the name of Jesus sounds
   In a believer's ear !
It soothes his sorrows, heals his wounds,
   And drives away his fear.

It makes the wounded spirit whole,
   And calms the troubled breast ;
'Tis manna to the hungry soul,
   And to the weary rest.

Dear name ! the rock on which I build,
   My shield and hiding place,
My never-failing treasury filled
   With boundless stores of grace.

Weak is the effort of my heart,
   And cold my warmest thought ;
But when I see Thee as Thou art,
   I'll praise Thee as I ought.

Till then I would my love proclaim
   With every fleeting breath ;
And may the music of Thy name
   Refresh my soul in death.

John Newton, 1779.

200

D. S. M.

REJOICE in Christ alway
When earth looks heavenly bright,
When joy makes glad the livelong day,
    And peace shuts in the night.
Rejoice when care and woe
The fainting soul oppress,
When tears at wakeful midnight flow,
    And morn brings heaviness.

Rejoice in hope and fear,
Rejoice in life and death,
Rejoice when threatening storms are near,
    And comfort languisheth.
When should they not rejoice
Whom Christ His brethren calls,
Who hear and know His guiding voice,
    As on their hearts it falls?

Yet not to rash excess
Let joy like ours prevail;
Feast not on earth's deliciousness,
    Till faith begin to fail.
Our temperate use of bliss,
    Let it to all appear;
And be our constant watchword this,
    " The Lord Himself is near."

201

(ECCLUS. L. 22—24.)

6. 7. 6. 7. 6. 6. 6. 6.

NOW thank we all our God,
With heart, and hands, and voices,
Who wondrous things hath done,
In whom His world rejoices ;
Who from our mother's arms
Hath blest us on our way
With countless gifts of love,
And still is ours to-day.

O may this bounteous God
Through all our life be near us,
With ever joyful hearts
And blessèd peace to cheer us ;
And keep us in His grace,
And guide us when perplext,
And free us from all ills
In this world and the next.

All praise and thanks to God,
The Father, now be given,
The Son, and Him who reigns
With them in highest heaven,
The One eternal God,
Whom earth and heaven adore,
For thus it was, is now,
And shall be evermore.

Catherine Winkworth, 1858,
from the German of Martin Rinckart, 1644.

202

P. M.

REJOICE to-day with one accord,
Sing out with exultation ;
Rejoice and praise our mighty Lord,
Whose Arm hath brought salvation ;
His works of love proclaim
The greatness of His Name ;
For He is God alone,
Who hath His mercy shown ;
Let all His saints adore Him !

When in distress to Him we cried,
He heard our sad complaining :
Oh, trust in Him, whate'er betide,
His love is all-sustaining ;
Triumphant songs of praise
To Him our hearts can raise ;
Now every voice shall say,
" Oh praise our God alway ! "
Let all His saints adore Him !

Rejoice to-day with one accord,
Sing out with exultation ;
Rejoice and praise our mighty Lord,
Whose Arm hath brought salvation ;
His works of love proclaim
The greatness of His Name ;
For He is God alone,
Who hath His mercy shown ;
Let all His saints adore Him !

Sir Henry W. Baker, 1861.

203

6. 6. 6. 6. 8. 8.

REJOICE, the Lord is King,
 Your Lord and King adore ;
Mortals, give thanks and sing,
 And triumph evermore ;
Lift up your heart, lift up your voice ;
Rejoice, again I say, Rejoice !

Jesus, the Saviour, reigns,
 The God of truth and love ;
When He had purged our stains,
 He took His seat above :
Lift up your heart, lift up your voice ;
Rejoice, again I say, Rejoice !

His kingdom cannot fail ;
 He rules o'er earth and heaven ;
The keys of death and hell
 Are to our Jesus given :
Lift up your heart, lift up your voice ;
Rejoice, again I say, Rejoice !

He sits at God's right hand
 Till all His foes submit,
And bow to His command,
 And fall beneath His feet ;
Lift up your heart, lift up your voice :
Rejoice, again I say, Rejoice !

Charles Wesley, 1746.

204

(Psalm CIII.)

8. 7. 8. 7. 4. 7.

PRAISE, my soul, the King of heaven ;
  To His feet thy tribute bring ;
Ransomed, healed, restored, forgiven,
  Who like me His praise should sing?
    Praise Him ! Praise Him !
  Praise the everlasting King !

Praise Him for His grace and favour
  To our fathers in distress ;
Praise Him still the same for ever,
  Slow to chide and swift to bless :
    Praise Him ! Praise Him !
  Glorious in His faithfulness !

Fatherlike, He tends and spares us,
  Well our feeble frame He knows ;
In His hand He gently bears us,
  Rescues us from all our foes :
    Praise Him ! Praise Him !
  Widely yet His mercy flows.

Angels, help us to adore Him ;
  Ye behold Him face to face :
Sun and moon, bow down before Him
  Dwellers all in time and space,
    Praise Him ! Praise Him !
  Praise with us the God of grace !

Henry F. Lyte, 1834.

205

(PSALM CL.)

Eight 7's.

PRAISE the Lord, His glories show,
Saints within His courts below,
Angels round His throne above,
All that see and share His love.
Earth to heaven, and heaven to earth,
Tell His wonders, sing His worth ;
Age to age, and shore to shore,
Praise Him, praise Him, evermore !

Praise the Lord, His mercies trace ;
Praise His providence and grace,
All that He for man hath done,
All He sends us through His Son :
Strings and voices, hands and hearts,
In the concert bear your parts ;
All that breathe, your Lord adore,
Praise Him, praise Him, evermore !

Henry F. Lyte, 1834.

206

(Psalm CXLVIII.)

D. 8. 7. 8. 7.

PRAISE the Lord! ye heavens, adore Him!
  Praise Him, angels, in the height!
Sun and moon, rejoice before Him;
  Praise Him, all ye stars and light!
Praise the Lord! for He hath spoken:
  Worlds His mighty voice obeyed;
Laws, which never shall be broken,
  For their guidance He hath made.

Praise the Lord! for He is glorious:
  Never shall His promise fail;
God hath made His saints victorious,
  Sin and death shall not prevail.
Praise the God of our salvation!
  Hosts on high, His power proclaim;
Heaven and earth, and all creation,
  Laud and magnify His name!

J. Kempthorne, 1809.

207

SONGS of praise the angels sang,
Heaven with hallelujahs rang,
When Jehovah's work begun,
When He spake and it was done.

Songs of praise awoke the morn,
When the Prince of Peace was born ;
Songs of praise arose, when He
Captive led Captivity.

Heaven and earth must pass away,
Songs of praise shall crown that day ;
God will make new heavens, new earth,
Songs of praise shall hail their birth.

And can man alone be dumb,
Till that glorious kingdom come ?
No ; the Church delights to raise
Psalms, and hymns, and songs of praise.

Saints below, with heart and voice,
Still in songs of praise rejoice,
Learning here by faith and love
Songs of praise to sing above.

Borne upon their latest breath,
Songs of praise shall conquer death ;
Then, amidst eternal joy,
Songs of praise their powers employ.

James Montgomery, 1819.

P

208

C. M.

COME, let us join our cheerful songs
  With angels round the throne ;
Ten thousand thousand are their tongues,
  But all their joys are one.

" Worthy the Lamb that died," they cry,
  " To be exalted thus ! "
" Worthy the Lamb," our lips reply,
  " For He was slain for us ! "

Jesus is worthy to receive
  Honour and power divine ;
And blessings, more than we can give,
  Be, Lord, for ever Thine.

Let all creation join in one
  To bless the sacred Name
Of Him that sits upon the throne,
  And to adore the Lamb !

Isaac Watts, 1709.

209

6. 6 7. 7. 7. 7. 6.

THERE was joy in heaven !
There was joy in heaven !
When this goodly world to frame
The Lord of might and mercy came ;
Shouts of joy were heard on high,
And the stars sang from the sky
  Glory to God in heaven !

There was joy in heaven !
There was joy in heaven !
When the billows, heaving dark,
Sank around the stranded ark,
And the rainbow's watery span
Spake of mercy, hope to man,
  And peace with God in heaven !

There was joy in heaven !
There was joy in heaven !
When of love the midnight beam
Dawned on the towers of Bethlehem ;
And along the echoing hill
Angels sang, " On earth goodwill,
  And glory in the heaven ! "

There is joy in heaven !
There is joy in heaven !
When the soul that went astray
Turns to Christ, the living way,
And, by grace of heaven subdued,
Breathes its prayer of gratitude,
  There is joy in heaven !

Bishop Heber, 1827.
P 2

210

D. 7. 6. 7. 6

GO when the morning shineth,
  Go when the noon is bright,
Go when the eve declineth,
  Go in the hush of night :
Go with pure mind and feeling,
  Fling earthly thoughts away,
And in thy chamber kneeling,
  Do thou in secret pray.

Remember all who love thee,
  All who are loved by thee ;
Pray too for those that hate thee,
  If any such there be :
Then for thyself in meekness
  A blessing humbly claim,
And link with each petition
  Thy great Redeemer's name.

But if 'tis e'er denied thee
  In solitude to pray ;
Should holy thoughts come o'er thee
  When friends are round thy way ;
E'en then the silent breathing
  Of thy spirit raised above
Shall reach His throne of glory,
  Of mercy, truth, and love.

Oh, not a joy or blessing
  With this can we compare,
The power that He hath given us
  To pour our souls in prayer.
Whene'er thou pin'st in sadness,
  Before His footstool fall ;
Remember in thy gladness
  His love who gave thee all.

Jane C. Simpson, 1831.

211

7. 7. 7. 3.

CHRISTIAN, seek not yet repose ;
Cast thy dreams of ease away ;
Thou art in the midst of foes :
     Watch and pray.

Gird thy heavenly armour on,
Wear it ever, night and day ;
Near thee lurks the evil one :
     Watch and pray.

Hear the warriors who o'ercame
Marching on their heavenward way,
Still with warning voice exclaim,
     Watch and pray.

First and chiefest, hear the Lord,
Him thou lovest to obey ;
Hide within thy heart His word :
     Watch and pray.

Watch, as if on thee alone
Hung the issue of the day ;
Pray, and all thy weakness own :
     Watch and pray.

Charlotte Elliott, 1836.

212

8. 7. 8. 7.

STRIVE aright when God doth call thee,
　When He draws thee by His grace ;
Cast off all that would enthral thee
　And deter thee from the race.

Combat, though thy life thou givest,
　Storm the Kingdom, but prevail ;
Let not Him with whom thou strivest
　Ever make thee faint or quail.

Wrestle till thy zeal is burning,
　And thy love is glowing warm,
All that earth can give thee spurning :
　Half love will not bide the storm.

Perfect truth will never waver,
　Wars with evil day and night,
Changes not for fear or favour,
　Only cares to win the fight.

Perfect truth will love to follow
　Watchfully our Master's ways ;
Seeks not comfort poor and hollow,
　Looks not for reward or praise.

Perfect truth from worldly pleasure,
　Worldly turmoil, stands apart ;
For in heaven is hid our treasure,
　There must also be the heart.

Soldiers of the Cross, take courage !
　Watch and war 'mid fear and pain ;
Daily conquering sin and sorrow,
　Till our King o'er earth shall reign.

Catherine Winkworth, 1862,
from the German of J. J. Winkler, 1703.

213

S. M.

BLEST are the pure in heart,
For they shall see our God ;
The secret of the Lord is theirs,
Their soul is Christ's abode.

The Lord who left the sky
Our life and peace to bring,
And dwelt in lowliness with men,
Their Pattern and their King,

Still to the lowly soul
He doth Himself impart,
And for His dwelling and His throne
Chooseth the pure in heart.

Lord, we Thy presence seek ;
May ours this blessing be !
Give us the pure and lowly heart,
A temple meet for Thee !

John Keble, 1819.

214

Four 6's.

WE name Thy name, O God,
  As our God call on Thee,
Though the dark heart meantime
  Far from Thy ways may be.

And we can own Thy law,
  And we can sing Thy songs,
While the sad inner soul
  To sin and shame belongs.

On us Thy love may glow
  As the pure mid-day fire,
On some foul spot look down,
  And yet the mire be mire.

Then spare us not Thy fires,
  The searching light and pain ;
Burn out our sin ; and, last,
  With Thy love heal again.

Francis T. Palgrave, 1862.

215

Four 7's

LORD, if Thou Thy grace impart,
Poor in spirit, meek in heart,
Like the Saviour we shall be,
Clothèd with humility.

Simple, teachable, and mild ;
Humble as a little child ;
Pleased with what the Lord provides,
Weaned from all the world besides.

Father, fix our souls on Thee :
Every evil let us flee ;
Always happy in Thy love,
Looking for our rest above.

All that seek will surely find
Every good in Christ combined ;
Oh, let Christians still adore,
Trust, and praise Him evermore !

Charles Wesley, 1741.

216

C. M.

THOU boundless source of every good,
  Our best desires fulfil ;
And help us to adore Thy grace,
  And mark Thy sovereign will.

In all Thy mercies may our souls
  Thy bounteous goodness see ;
Nor let the gifts Thy hand imparts
  Estrange our hearts from Thee.

In every changing scene of life,
  Whate'er that scene may be,
Give us a meek and humble mind,
  A mind at peace with Thee.

Do Thou direct our steps aright ;
  Help us Thy Name to fear ;
And give us grace to watch and pray,
  And strength to persevere.

Ottiwell Heginbotham, 1794.

217

L. M.

O HOLY Lord, content to live
  In a poor home, a lowly child,
And in subjection meek to give
  Obedience to Thy mother mild :

Lead every child that bears Thy name
  To walk in Thy pure upright way,
To dread the touch of sin and shame,
  And humbly, like Thyself, obey !

O let not this world's scorching glow
  Thy Spirit's quickening dew efface,
Nor blast of sin too rudely blow,
  And quench the trembling flame of grace.

Gather Thy lambs within Thine arm,
  And gently in Thy bosom bear ;
Keep them, O Lord, from hurt and harm,
  And bid them rest for ever there !

So shall they, waiting here below
  Like Thee, their Lord, a little span,
In wisdom and in stature grow,
  And favour both with God and man.

William W. How, 1854.

218

(Psalm CXXXIX.)

L. M.

THOU, Lord, by strictest search hast known
My rising up, and lying down :
My secret thoughts are known to Thee,
Known long before conceived by me.

Thine eye my bed and path surveys,
My public haunts and private ways :
Thou knowest all my lips would vent,
My yet unuttered words' intent.

Surrounded by Thy power I stand,
On every side I feel Thy hand :
O skill for human reach too high,
Too dazzling bright for mortal eye !

Search, prove, O Lord, my thoughts and heart.
If sin yet lurk in any part :
Correct me where I go astray,
And guide me in Thy perfect way.

Tate and Brady, 1696.

2I9

(Psalm CXIX.)

C. M.

HOW shall the young preserve their ways
　From all pollution free ?
By making still their course of life
　With God's commands agree.

With hearty zeal for Thee we seek,
　To Thee for succour pray ;
Lord, suffer not our careless steps
　From Thy right paths to stray !

Safe in our heart, and closely hid,
　Thy word, our treasure, lies ;
To succour us with timely aid
　When sinful thoughts arise.

Secured by that, our grateful souls
　Shall ever bless Thy name ;
O teach us then by Thy just laws
　Our future life to frame !

Tate and Brady, 1696.

220

L. M.

O THOU, who hast at Thy command
The hearts of all men in Thy hand ;
Our wayward, erring hearts incline
To know no other will but Thine.

Our wishes, our designs control ;
Mould every purpose of the soul ;
O'er all may we victorious be,
That stands between ourselves and Thee.

Twice blest will all our blessings be
When we can look from them to Thee ;
When each glad heart its tribute pays
Of love, and gratitude, and praise.

Yet may we, feeble, weak and frail,
Against our mightiest foes prevail ;
Thy word our shield from every harm,
Our strength Thine everlasting arm.

Thomas Cotterill, 1810.

221

8. 7. 8. 7. 7. 7.

LORD, who once from heaven descending
  Lost mankind didst seek and save,
Us in our distress befriending,
  Grant the succour which we crave ;
From a sinful world we flee,
Shepherd of our souls, to Thee.

From the arts which would allure us,
  From the toils that would ensnare,
Thou who slumberest not, secure us,
  By Thy ever watchful care :
And if e'er from Thee we roam,
Fetch, O fetch the wanderers home !

And at last, our perils ended,
  Take us to that blessed fold,
Where the flock Thou here hast tended
  Shall in heaven Thy face behold,
And with songs of praise adore
Christ their Shepherd evermore.

Latham.

222

P. M.

LEAD us, heavenly Father, lead us,
  O'er the world's tempestuous sea ;
Guard us, guide us, keep us, feed us,
  For we have no help but Thee ;
      Yet possessing
      Every blessing
  If our God our Father be.

Saviour, breathe forgiveness o'er us ;
  All our weakness Thou dost know :
Thou didst tread this earth before us,
  Thou didst feel its keenest woe ;
      Lone and dreary,
      Faint and weary,
  Through the desert Thou didst go.

Spirit of our God, descending,
  Fill our hearts with heavenly joy :
Love with every passion blending,
  Pleasure that can never cloy ;
      Thus provided,
      Pardoned, guided,
  Nothing can our peace destroy.

James Edmeston, 1820.

223

7. 6. 7. 6. 8. 7. 6.

O THOU, of God the Father,
　The true eternal Son,
Of whom 'tis surely written
　That Thou with Him art one ;
Thou art the bright and morning Star,
　Beyond all other radiance
　　Thy glory streams afar.

O let us in Thy knowledge
　And in Thy love increase,
That we in faith be steadfast
　And serve Thee here in peace !
That so Thy sweetness may be known
　To these cold hearts, and teach them
　　To thirst for Thee alone.

Maker of all ! who showest
　The Father's love and might,
In heaven and earth Thou reignest
　Of Thine own power and right ;
So rule our hearts and minds, that we
　Be wholly Thine, and never
　　May turn aside from Thee !

Catherine Winkworth, 1862,
from the German of Elizabeth Creutziger, 1524.

Q

224

C. M.

BE Thou my Guardian and my Guide,
　And hear me when I call;
Let not my slippery footsteps slide,
　And hold me lest I fall.

The world, the flesh, and Satan dwell
　Around the path I tread;
O save me from the snares of hell,
　Thou Quickener of the dead.

And if I tempted am to sin,
　And outward things are strong,
Do Thou, O Lord, keep watch within,
　And save my soul from wrong.

Still let me ever watch and pray,
　And feel that I am frail;
That if the tempter cross my way,
　Yet he may not prevail.

Isaac Williams, ✠ 1865.

225

(GEN. XXVIII. 20—22.)

C. M.

O GOD of Israel ! by whose hand
  Thy people still are fed ;
Who through this weary pilgrimage
  Hast all our fathers led ;

Our vows, our prayers, we now present
  Before Thy throne of grace :
God of our fathers ! be the God
  Of their succeeding race.

Through each perplexing path of life
  Our wandering footsteps guide ;
Give us each day our daily bread,
  Our heavenly food provide.

O spread Thy covering wings around,
  Till all our wanderings cease,
And at our Father's loved abode
  Our souls arrive in peace.

Such blessings from Thy gracious hand
  Our humble prayers implore ;
That Thou mayst be our chosen God,
  And portion evermore.

Variation by John Logan, 1781,
from Philip Doddridge, 1737.

Q 2

226

Six 8's.

O KING of kings, before whose throne
  The Angels bow, no gift can we
Present that is indeed our own,
  Since heaven and earth belong to Thee :
Yet this our souls through grace impart,
The offering of a thankful heart.

O Jesu, set at God's right hand,
  With Thine eternal Father plead
For all Thy loyal-hearted band,
  Who still on earth Thy succour need ;
For them in weakness strength provide,
And through the world their footsteps guide.

O Holy Spirit, Fount of breath,
  Whose comforts never fail nor fade,
Vouchsafe the life that knows no death,
  Vouchsafe the light that knows no shade ;
And grant that we through all our days
May share Thy gifts, and sing Thy praise.

Variation by Thomas Darling, 1857,
from John Quarles, 1654.

227

C. M.

ABIDE among us with Thy grace,
   Lord Jesus, evermore,
Nor let us e'er to sin give place,
   Nor grieve Him we adore.

Abide among us with Thy word,
   Redeemer, whom we love ;
Thy help and mercy here afford,
   And life with Thee above.

Abide with us to bless us still,
   O bounteous Lord of Peace ;
With grace and power our spirits fill,
   Our faith and love increase.

Abide among us as our shield,
   O Captain of Thy host ;
That to the world we may not yield,
   Nor e'er forsake our post.

Abide with us in faithful love,
   Our God and Saviour be,
Thy help at need O let us prove,
   And keep us true to Thee.

*Catherine Winkworth, 1858,
from the German of Stegmann, 1629.*

228

C. M.

O FOR a heart to praise my God !
　A heart from sin set free !
A heart that's sprinkled with the blood
　So freely shed for me !

A heart resigned, submissive, meek,
　My great Redeemer's throne ;
Where only Christ is heard to speak,
　Where Jesus reigns alone !

A humble, lowly, contrite heart,
　Believing, true, and clean ;
Which neither life nor death can part
　From Him that dwells within !

A heart in every thought renewed,
　And full of love divine ;
Perfect, and right, and pure, and good—
　A copy, Lord, of Thine !

Thy nature, gracious Lord, impart ;
　Come quickly from above ;
Write Thy new name upon my heart,
　Thy new best name of Love.

Charles Wesley, 1742.

229

Four 7's.

JESUS, Lord, we look to Thee,
Let us in Thy name agree ;
Show Thyself the Prince of Peace ;
Bid all strife for ever cease.

By Thy reconciling love
Every stumbling-block remove ;
Each to each unite, endear ;
Come, and spread Thy banner here !

Make us of one heart and mind,
Courteous, pitiful, and kind,
Lowly, meek, in thought and word,
Altogether like our Lord.

Let us each for other care,
Each his brother's burdens bear ;
To the world a pattern give,
Show how Christ's disciples live.

Take us to Thy home above,
Purified by faith and love ;
May we in our life's last hour
Feel Thy peace, Thy grace, Thy power.

Altered from Charles Wesley, 1743.

230

L. M.

JESUS, where'er Thy people meet,
There they behold Thy mercy-seat ;
Where'er they seek Thee, Thou art found,
And every place is hallowed ground.

For Thou, within no walls confined,
Inhabitest the humble mind ;
Such ever bring Thee where they come,
And going take Thee to their home.

Dear Shepherd of Thy faithful few,
Thy former mercies here renew ;
Here to our waiting souls proclaim
The sweetness of Thy saving Name.

Here may we prove the power of prayer
To strengthen faith and sweeten care ;
To teach our faint desires to rise,
And bring all heaven before our eyes.

Lord, we are few, but Thou art near ;
Nor short Thine arm, nor deaf Thine ear :
O, rend the heavens, come quickly down,
And make a thousand hearts thine own.

William Cowper, 1769.

231

C. M.

LORD, when we bend before Thy throne,
 And our confessions pour,
Teach us to feel the sins we own,
 And hate what we deplore.

Our broken spirits pitying see ;
 True penitence impart ;
Then let a kindling glance from Thee
 Beam hope upon the heart.

When we disclose our wants in prayer
 May we our wills resign,
And not a thought our bosoms share
 Which is not wholly Thine.

Let faith each meek petition fill,
 And lift it to the skies ;
And teach our hearts 'tis goodness still
 Which grants it or denies.

When our united voices strive
 Their cheerful hymns to raise,
Let love divine within us live,
 And lift our souls in praise.

Then on Thy glories while we dwell,
 Thy mercies we'll review,
Till love divine transported tell
 Thou, God, art Father too !

Joseph D. Carlyle, 1805.

232

6. 5. 6. 5.

JESU, meek and gentle,
  Son of God most high,
Pitying, loving Saviour,
  Hear Thy children's cry.

Pardon our offences,
  Loose our captive chains,
Break down every idol
  Which our soul detains.

Give us holy freedom,
  Fill our hearts with love ;
Draw us, holy Jesus !
  To the realms above.

Lead us on our journey,
  Be Thyself the Way
Through terrestrial darkness
  To celestial day.

Jesu, meek and gentle,
  Son of God most high,
Pitying, loving Saviour,
  Hear Thy children's cry.

George R. Prynne, 1856.

233

(Psalm CXXXVII.)

S. M.

FAR from my heavenly home,
Far from my Father's breast,
Fainting I cry, " Blest Spirit, come,
And speed me to my rest."

My spirit homeward turns,
And fain would thither flee ;
My heart, O Zion, droops and yearns,
When I remember thee.

To thee, to thee I press,
A dark and toilsome road ;
When shall I pass the wilderness,
And reach the saints' abode?

God of my life, be near ;
On Thee my hopes I cast ;
O guide me through the desert here,
And bring me home at last.

Henry F. Lyte, 1834.

234

L. M.

O THOU, who camest from above
 The pure celestial fire to impart,
Kindle a flame of sacred love
 On the mean altar of my heart.

Then let it for Thy glory burn
 With inextinguishable blaze ;
And, trembling, to its source return,
 In humble prayer and fervent praise.

Jesus ! confirm my heart's desire
 To work, and speak, and think for Thee ;
Still let me guard the holy fire,
 And still stir up Thy gift in me :

Ready for all Thy perfect will,
 My acts of faith and love repeat :
Till death Thy endless mercies seal,
 And make my sacrifice complete.

      Charles Wesley, 1762.

235

L. M.

O GOD, I long Thy light to see ;
My God, I hourly think on Thee ;
O draw me up, nor hide Thy face,
But help me from Thy holy place.

Ah, how shall I my freedom win ?
How break this heavy yoke of sin ?
My fainting spirit thirsts for Thee ;
Come, Lord, to help and set me free.

My heart is set to do Thy will,
But all my deeds are faulty still ;
My best attempts are nothing worth,
But soiled with cleaving taint of earth.

Fain would my heart henceforward be
Fixed, O my God, alone on Thee,
That heart and soul by Thee possest
May find in Thee their perfect rest.

O take away whate'er has stood
Between me and the Highest Good ;
I ask no better boon than this,
To find in God my only bliss.

Catherine Winkworth, 1855,
from the German of Anton Ulrich,
Duke of Brunswick, 1667.

236

Six 8's.

JESU, my Lord, my God, my All,
Hear me, blest Saviour, when I call ;
Hear me, and from Thy dwelling-place
Pour down the riches of Thy grace.
    Jesu, my Lord, I Thee adore ;
    O make me love Thee more and more.

Jesu, too late I Thee have sought ;
How can I love Thee as I ought ?
And how extol Thy matchless fame,
The glorious beauty of Thy Name ?
    Jesu, my Lord, I Thee adore ;
    O make me love Thee more and more.

Jesu, what didst Thou find in me,
That Thou hast dealt so lovingly ?
How great the joy that Thou hast brought,
So far exceeding hope or thought !
    Jesu, my Lord, I Thee adore ;
    O make me love Thee more and more.

Jesu, of Thee shall be my song,
To Thee my heart and soul belong ;
All that I am or have is Thine,
And Thou, blest Saviour, Thou art mine.
    Jesu, my Lord, I Thee adore ;
    O make me love Thee more and more.

Henry Collins. 1852.

237

C. M.

TRY us, O God ! and search the ground
   Of every evil heart :
Whate'er of sin in us is found,
   O bid it all depart.

When to the right or left we stray,
   Pity Thy helpless sheep ;
Bring back our feet into the way,
   And there Thy wanderers keep.

Help us to help each other, Lord,
   Each other's cross to bear ;
Let each his friendly aid afford
   To soothe his brother's care.

Help us to build each other up,
   Help us ourselves to prove ;
Increase our faith, confirm our hope,
   And perfect us in love.

Complete at length Thy work of grace,
   And take us to Thy rest,
Among the saints who see Thy face,
   To be for ever blest.

Charles Wesley, 1743.

238

Eight 7's.

THOU hast gone before us, Lord,
Not with anger, strife, or sword,
Not with kingly pomp and pride,
But with mercy at Thy side.
Moved by wondrous love divine
For our life Thou gavest Thine.
And Thy precious outpoured blood
Won for us the highest good.

Let us follow in such sort,
Christ-like every deed and thought,
That Thy love most true and kind
All our hearts henceforth may bind ;
None may look behind him now,
Who to Christ hath pledged his vow ;
Jesus leads, no longer stand ;
" Follow me" is His command.

Draw me up, my God, from hence,
Raise me high o'er earth and sense,
That I lose not Thee from sight,
Nor in life nor death, my Light.
In my soul's most deep recess
Let me cherish holiness,
Not for show or human praise,
But for Thy sake, all my days.

Grant me, Lord, my heart's desire,
So my course to run nor tire,
That my practised soul may prove
What Thy meekness, what Thy love.
Grant me here to trust Thy grace,
There with joy to see Thy face,
This in time my portion be ;
That through all eternity !

Catherine Winkworth, 1855,
from the German of Ris!, 1644.

239

C. M.

" COME to a desert-place apart,
    And rest a little while ; "
So spake the Lord, when limbs and heart
    Waxed faint and sick through toil.

What tired nature craved He sought,
    But, while He sought it, found
The restless crowd together brought,
    And labour's weary round.

Still not a thought to self was given,
    Nor murmur from Him came ;
He fed their souls with bread from heaven,
    And stayed their sinking frame ;

Nor turned, when that long task was done,
    To sleep fatigue away ;
When on the desert sank the sun,
    The Saviour waked to pray.

O perfect Pattern from above !
    So strengthen us, that ne'er
Prayer keep us back from works of love,
    Nor works of love from prayer.

Bishop Woodford, 1853,
    from the Latin.

240

L. M.

BE with me, Lord, where'er I go,
Teach me what Thou wouldst have me do,
Suggest whate'er I think or say,
Direct me in Thy narrow way.

Prevent me, lest I harbour pride,
Lest I in my own strength confide ;
Show me my weakness, let me see
I have my power, my all, from Thee.

Assist and teach me how to pray,
Incline my nature to obey ;
What Thou abhorrest let me flee,
And only love what pleases Thee.

John Cennick, 1752.

241

Four 7's.

GOD of mercy, throned on high,
  Listen from Thy lofty seat ;
Hear, O hear our feeble cry,
  Guide, O guide our wandering feet !

Young and erring travellers, we
  All our dangers do not know ;
Scarcely fear the stormy sea,
  Hardly feel the tempest blow.

Jesus, lover of the young,
  Cleanse us with Thy blood divine ;
Ere the tide of sin grow strong,
  Save us, keep us, make us Thine.

When perplexed in danger's snare,
  Thou alone our Guide canst be ;
When oppressed with woe and care,
  Whom have we to trust but Thee ?

Let us ever hear Thy voice,
  Ask Thy counsel every day ;
Saints and angels will rejoice
  If we walk in wisdom's way.

Saviour, give us faith, and pour
  Hope and love on every soul ;
Hope, till time shall be no more ;
  Love, while endless ages roll !

Neele, 1833.

D. 8. 7. 8. 7.

LIGHT of those whose dreary dwelling
  Borders on the shades of death,
Come, and, all Thy love revealing,
  Dissipate the clouds beneath.
Thou, new heaven and earth's Creator,
  On our deepest darkness rise,
Scattering all the night of nature,
  Pouring light on blinded eyes.

Still we wait for Thine appearing;
  Life and joy Thy beams impart :
Chasing all our fears, and cheering
  Every poor, benighted heart.
By Thy all restoring merit,
  Every burdened soul release ;
Every weary, wandering spirit
  Guide into Thy perfect peace.

Charles Wesley, 1745.

243 S. 7. S. 7. + 7.

JESUS, Lord, we kneel before Thee,
  Bend from heaven Thy gracious ear ;
While our waiting souls adore Thee,
  Friend of helpless sinners, hear :
    By Thy mercy,
  O deliver us, good Lord.

From the depths of nature's blindness,
  From the hardening power of sin,
From all malice and unkindness,
  From the pride that lurks within,
    By Thy mercy, &c.

When temptation sorely presses,
  In the day of Satan's power,
In our time of deep distresses,
  In each dark and trying hour,
    By Thy mercy, &c.

When the world around is smiling,
  In the time of wealth and ease,
Earthly joys our hearts beguiling,
  In the day of health and peace,
    By Thy mercy, &c.

In the weary hours of sickness,
  In the times of grief and pain,
When we feel our mortal weakness,
  When the creature's help is vain,
    By Thy mercy, &c.

In the solemn hour of dying,
  In the awful judgment day,
May our souls, on Thee relying,
  Find Thee still our hope and stay :
    By Thy mercy,
  O deliver us, good Lord.
         James J. Cummins, 1849.

244

8. 7. 8. 7. 8. 8.

THOUGH we long, in sin-wrought blindness,
  From Thy gracious paths have strayed,
Cold to Thee and to Thy kindness,
  Wilful, reckless, or afraid ;
Through dim clouds that gather round us
Thou hast sought, and Thou hast found us.

Oft from Thee we veil our faces,
  Children-like, to cheat Thine eyes ;
Sin, and hope to hide the traces ;
  From ourselves ourselves disguise :
'Neath the webs we've woven round us
Thy soul-piercing glance has found us.

Sudden, midst our idle chorus,
  O'er our sin Thy thunders roll ;
Death his signal waves before us,
  Night and terror take the soul ;
Till through double darkness round us
Looks a star,—and Thou hast found us.

O most Merciful, most Holy,
  Light Thy wanderers on their way ;
Keep us ever Thine, Thine wholly,
  Suffer us no more to stray !
Cloud and storm oft gather round us :
We were lost, but Thou hast found us.

Francis T. Palgrave, 1862.

245

8. 7. 8. 7. 4. 7.

GUIDE us, O Thou great Jehovah !
  Pilgrims through this barren land ;
We are weak, but Thou art mighty,
  Hold us with Thy powerful hand :
    Bread of heaven,
  Feed us now and evermore.

Open Thou the living fountain
  Whence the healing waters flow ;
Let the fiery cloudy pillar
  Lead us all our journey through ;
    Strong Deliverer,
  Be Thou still our strength and shield.

When we tread the verge of Jordan,
  Bid our anxious fears subside !
Bear us through th' o'erwhelming torrent,
  Lead us safe to Canaan's side :
    Songs of praises
  We will ever give to Thee.

From the Welsh of William Williams, 1774.

246

D. 8. 8. 6.

WHILE we in supplication join,
Before the throne of grace divine,
   In mercy bow Thine ear ;
And while we listen to Thy word,
Or praise Thy name with glad accord,
   Amongst us, Lord, appear.

The veil that hides Thy glory rend ;
In love and saving power descend,
   To visit Thine abode ;
Here to each heart Thy grace reveal,
And all who enter cause to feel
   The presence of our God.

John Walker.

247

8. 7. 8. 7. 4. 7.

LORD, dismiss us with Thy blessing,
 Fill our hearts with joy and peace ;
Let us each, Thy love possessing,
 Triumph in redeeming grace ;
  O refresh us,
 Travelling through this wilderness !

Thanks we give, and adoration,
 For Thy gospel's joyful sound ;
May the fruits of Thy salvation,
 In our hearts and lives abound !
  May Thy presence
 With us evermore be found !

So whene'er the signal's given
 Us from earth to call away,
Borne on angels' wings to heaven,
 Glad the summons to obey,
  May we ever
 Reign with Thee in endless day !

Hon. Walter Shirley, 1774.

C. M.

GREAT Shepherd of Thy people, hear ;
   Thy presence now display :
As Thou hast given a place for prayer,
   So give us hearts to pray.

Within these walls let holy peace
   And love and concord dwell :
Here give the troubled conscience ease,
   The wounded spirit heal.

May we in faith receive Thy word,
   In faith present our prayers,
And in the presence of our Lord
   Unbosom all our cares.

The hearing ear, the seeing eye,
   The contrite heart, bestow ;
And shine upon us from on high,
   That we in grace may grow.

John Newton, 1779.

249

C. M.

ETERNAL God, we look to Thee,
    To Thee for help we fly ;
Thine eye alone our wants can see,
    Thy hand alone supply.

From path to path we roam for rest,
    But all our search is vain ;
We seek for life among the dead,
    For joy where sorrows reign.

Lord, let Thy fear within us dwell,
    Thy love our footsteps guide :
That love will all vain love expel ;
    That fear, all fear beside.

Not what we wish, but what we want,
    O let Thy grace supply :
The good unasked in mercy grant ;
    The ill, though asked, deny.

James Merrick, 1765.

250

C. M.

FATHER of mercies ! let our ways
  With Thee acceptance find ;
Thy loving-kindness we confess
  To us and all mankind.

Thanks for creation are Thy due,
  For life preserved by Thee ;
And all the blessings life affords,
  So great and yet so free.

Thanks for redemption, above all,
  To us in Jesus given ;
Thanks for the means of grace on earth,
 . And for the hope of heaven.

O let a sense of this Thy grace
  Our best affections move ;
That while our lips Thy praise proclaim
  Our hearts may feel Thy love.

251

8. 6. 8. 6. 8. 8. 8. 8.

OUR Father, guide those streams aright
  Which have their springs in Thee ;
Shine on them with Thy heavenly light,
  And make them pure and free.
And ever, as they onward flow
Through all the darkling scenes below,
May they reflect that Heaven above,
Which looks on us in perfect love !

Sin ever would enchain the heart,
  But Christ has made us free ;
And He would bid those fears depart
  Which draw our hearts from Thee.
Thou art our Father ; Thou hast known
Our wayward thoughts ; in Thee alone
Is all our fulness, all our joy,
Those pleasures which can never cloy.

Thou knowest all our seasons too,
  Their ever-varying tone :
Refresh us with the morning dew,
  Nor let our night be lone.
At noonday let the showers fall,
In answer to our suppliant call ;
Strengthen our hearts, and hold us fast,
That we may praise Thee to the last.

E. S., 1849.

P. M.

WITH trembling awe the chosen three
  The holy mount ascended,
Where, wrapped in blissful ecstasy,
  They saw the vision splendid—
Their Lord arrayed in living light,
And on His left hand and His right
  By glorious saints attended.

O vision bright—too bright to tell—
  The joys of heaven unveiling !
How precious on those hearts it fell,
  When earthly hopes were failing ;
When, saints no more on either side,
Between the thieves the Saviour died,
  'Mid hate and scorn and railing !

Grant us, dear Lord, some vision brief
  Of future triumph telling,
Gilding with hope our night of grief,
  Our clouds of fear dispelling.
If the dim foretaste was so bright,
Oh, what shall be the dazzling light
  Of Thy eternal dwelling !

William W. How, 1860.

253

Four 7's.

WONDROUS was Thy path on earth,
'Midst our human grief and mirth,
All our good, and all our ill
Feeling, Lord, yet sinless still.

Thou wouldst oft vouchsafe to bless
Hours of earthly happiness ;
When Thou cam'st Thy friend to save,
Thou couldst weep beside his grave.

Thy transforming influence still
Into good converts our ill ;
Or from weak and worthless things
Holy joy and comfort brings.

O be with us, gracious Lord !
Near our bed. and at our board,
By our fireside's pleasant cheer,
When the winter nights are drear.

Through the livelong summer day,
When our hearts are blithe and gay,
From all taint of fleshly ill
Purify our gladness still.

So that when new heavens and earth
At Thy bidding shall have birth,
Purged from all our dross of sin,
We may dwell with Thee therein.

S. M.

OH, where shall rest be found,
    Rest for the weary soul ?
'Twere vain the ocean's depths to sound,
    Or pierce to either pole.

The world can never give
    The bliss for which we sigh ;
'Tis not the whole of life to live,
    Nor all of death to die.

Beyond this vale of tears
    There is a life above,
Unmeasured by the flight of years,
    And all that life is love.

There is a death whose pang
    Outlasts the fleeting breath ;
Oh, what eternal horrors hang
    Around the second death !

Lord God of truth and grace,
    Teach us that death to shun,
Lest we be banished from Thy face,
    And evermore undone.

James Montgomery, 1819.

255

L. M.

LET me be with Thee where Thou art,
  My Saviour, my eternal Rest !
Then only will this longing heart
  Be fully and for ever blest.

Let me be with Thee where Thou art,
  Thy unveiled glory to behold ;
Then only will this wandering heart
  Cease to be treacherous, faithless, cold.

Let me be with Thee where Thou art,
  Where spotless saints Thy Name adore ;
Then only will this sinful heart
  Be evil and defiled no more.

Let me be with Thee where Thou art,
  Where none can die, where none remove ;
There neither death nor life will part
  Me from Thy presence and Thy love.

Charlotte Elliott, 1836.

256

Six 7's.

LORD of power and Lord of might,
God and Father of us all,
Lord of day and Lord of night,
Listen to our solemn call :
Listen, whilst to Thee we raise
Songs of prayer and songs of praise.

Light and love and life are Thine,
Great Creator of all good,
Fill our souls with light divine,
Give us with our daily food
Blessings from Thy heavenly store,
Blessings rich for evermore.

Full of love and full of peace,
May our life on earth be blest ;
When our trials here shall cease,
And at last we sink to rest,
Fountain of eternal love !
Call us to our home above.

Godfrey Thring, 1866.

257

C. M.

FATHER, whate'er of earthly bliss
　Thy sovereign will denies,
Accepted at Thy throne of grace
　Let this petition rise.

Give me a calm, a thankful heart,
　From every murmur free ;
The blessings of Thy grace impart,
　And let me live to Thee.

Let the sweet hope that Thou art mine
　My life and death attend ;
Thy presence through my journey shine,
　And crown my journey's end.

Anne Steele, 1760.

258

D. 8. 7. 8. 7.

LOVE Divine, all love excelling,
  Joy of heaven, to earth come down,
Fix in us Thy humble dwelling,
  All Thy faithful mercies crown.
Jesus, Thou art all compassion,
  Pure, unbounded love Thou art :
Visit us with Thy salvation,
  Enter every longing heart.

Come, Almighty to deliver,
  Let us all Thy grace receive ;
Suddenly return, and never—
  Never more Thy temples leave.
Thee we would be always blessing,
  Serve Thee as Thy hosts above ;
Pray and praise Thee without ceasing,
  Glory in Thy perfect love.

Finish, then, Thy new creation,
  Pure, unspotted may we be :
Let us see Thy great salvation
  Perfectly restored by Thee :
Changed from glory into glory,
  Till in heaven we take our place,
Till we cast our crowns before Thee,
  Lost in wonder, love, and praise.

Charles Wesley, 1743.

259

(PSALM XC.)

D. 8. 8. 6.

O GOD of glory, God of grace,
From age to age our dwelling-place,
   Before Thy throne we bow :
Ere the vast mountains rose of yore,
When they and earth shall be no more,
   The same, O Lord, art Thou.

Man's generations rise and pass :
Like morning flowers, like summer grass,
   The creatures of Thy breath :
Our life runs onward like a stream,
We come and vanish as a dream,
   The prey of sin and death.

Unnumbered ills beset our path,
Our days are darkened 'neath Thy wrath,
   And yet how heedless we !
O touch with grace each erring heart,
True wisdom to each soul impart,
   And win us all to Thee.

We sink, we perish 'neath Thy frown :
O send Thy healing mercy down
   To light our coming years ;
Then be they many, be they few,
Thy grace will bear us safely through
   Beyond the reach of tears.

Henry F. Lyte, 1847.

260

D. C. M.

THE roseate hues of early dawn,
  The brightness of the day,
The crimson of the sunset sky,
  How fast they fade away !
O for the pearly gates of heaven !
  O for the golden floor !
O for the Sun of Righteousness
  That setteth nevermore !

The highest hopes we cherish here,
  How fast they tire and faint !
How many a spot defiles the robe
  That wraps an earthly saint !
O for a heart that never sins,
  O for a soul washed white !
O for a voice to praise our King,
  Nor weary day or night !

Here faith is ours, and heavenly hope,
  And grace to lead us higher ;
But there are perfectness and peace
  Beyond our best desire.
O by Thy love and anguish, Lord !
  O by Thy life laid down !
O that we fall not from Thy grace,
  Nor cast away our crown !

              Cecil F. Alexander, 1853.

261

C. M.

POUR down Thy Spirit, gracious Lord,
  On all assembled here :
Let us receive the engrafted Word
  With meekness and with fear.

By faith in Thee the soul receives
  New life, though dead before ;
And he, who in Thy name believes,
  Shall live, to die no more.

Preserve the power of faith alive
  In those that love Thy name ;
For sin and Satan daily strive
  To quench the sacred flame.

Thy grace and mercy first prevailed
  From death to set us free ;
And often since, our life had failed
  Unless renewed by Thee.

To Thee we look, to Thee we bow,
  To Thee for help we call,
Our Life and Resurrection Thou,
  Our Hope, our Joy, our All.

John Newton, 1779.

262

Six 8's.

LEAVE God to order all thy ways,
 And hope in Him whate'er betide,
Thou'lt find Him in the evil days
 Thy all-sufficient strength and guide :
Who trusts in God's unchanging love
Builds on the rock that nought can move.

Only thy restless heart keep still,
 And wait in cheerful hope ; content
To take whate'er His gracious will,
 His all-discerning love hath sent ;
Nor doubt our inmost wants are known
To Him who chose us for His own.

He knows when joyful hours are best,
 He sends them as He sees it meet ;
When thou hast borne the fiery test,
 And now art freed from all deceit,
He comes to thee all unaware,
And makes thee own His loving care.

Sing, pray, and swerve not from His ways,
 But do thine own part faithfully,
Trust His rich promises of grace,
 So shall they be fulfilled in thee :
God never yet forsook at need
The soul that trusted Him indeed.

*Catherine Winkworth, 1855,
from the German of George Neumark, 1653.*

263

P. M.

CEASE, my soul, thy tribulation,
  Banish all thy griefs and fears ;
Christ in whom is thy salvation
  Calls thee from the vale of tears.
From the desert where we roam
He will lead the wanderers home
Unto joys all joys transcending,
Unto peace that knows no ending.

Light me, O Thou Star uprising,
  Jesus, all my glory be ;
So will I, the shame despising,
  Take my cross and follow Thee.
Help me with Thy presence blest,
Till I gain the perfect rest ;
Till the grave's dark gate enfold me,
With Thy word assure, uphold me.

Trusting in Thy love so tender,
  I will bear the bitter strife ;
Glad to Thee my soul surrender,
  Death shall be the path of life.
Thou who openedst Paradise
To the dying sinner's eyes,
Jesus, Thou wilt never leave me,
But to Thy great light receive me.

Cease, my soul, thy tribulation,
  Banish all thy griefs and fears ;
Christ in whom is thy salvation
  Calls thee from the vale of tears.
Soon before Him shalt thou stand,
Where the saints, a ransomed band,
At His feet their crowns are casting
In the glory everlasting.

Thomas E. Brown, 1872,
from the German of Simon Graf.

264

D. 8. 7. 8. 7.

WHO puts his trust in God most just
    Hath built his house securely ;
He who relies on Jesus Christ,
    Heaven shall be his most surely ;
Then fixed on Thee my trust shall be,
    For Thy truth cannot alter ;
While mine Thou art, not death's worst smart
    Shall make my courage falter.

Though fiercest foes my course oppose,
    A dauntless front I'll show them ;
My champion Thou, Lord Christ, art now,
    Who soon shalt overthrow them !
And if but Thee I have in me
    With Thy good gifts and Spirit,
Nor death nor hell, I know full well,
    Shall hurt me, through Thy merit.

I rest me here without a fear,
    By Thee shall all be given
That I can need, O faithful God,
    For this life or for heaven.
O make me true, my heart renew,
    My soul and flesh deliver !
Lord, hear my prayer, and in Thy care
    Keep me in peace for ever.

Catherine Winkworth, 1858,
from the German of (probably) Joachim
Magdeburg, ✠ 1560.

265

D. S. M.

IF God be on my side,
  Then let who will oppose,
For oft ere now to Him I cried,
  And He hath quelled my foes.
  If Jesus be my Friend,
  If God doth love me well,
What matters all my foes intend,
  Though strong they be and fell ?

Here I can firmly rest,
  I dare to boast of this,
That God, the highest and the best,
  My Friend and Father is.
  From dangerous snares He saves ;
  Where'er He bids me go,
He checks the storms and calms the waves,
  That nought can work me woe.

His Spirit in me dwells,
  O'er all my mind He reigns,
All care and sadness He dispels,
  And soothes away all pains.
  He prospers day by day
  His work within my heart,
Till I have strength and faith to say,
  Thou, God, my Father art !

Catherine Winkworth, 1855,
from the German of Paul Gerhardt, 1650.

266

Six 8's.

CAPTAIN of Israel's host, and Guide
  Of all who seek their home above,
Beneath Thy shadow we abide,
  The cloud of Thy protecting love ;
Our strength, Thy grace ; our rule, Thy word ;
Our end, the glory of the Lord.

By Thine unerring Spirit led,
  We shall not in the desert stray ;
By Thy paternal bounty fed,
  We shall not want in all our way ;
As far from danger as from fear,
While love, Almighty love, is near.

Altered from Charles Wesley, 1753.

267

8. 7. 8. 7. 8. 8. 7.

A TOWER of strength our God doth stand,
  A Shield and sure Defender:
True help from all our woes His hand
  Through life doth freely render.
Our foe hath fixed his purpose fell;
With might and craft he's armed full well;
  Nought earthly can resist him.

Full soon we're lost and vanquished quite,
  Our strength hath nought effected;
Yet He for us maintains the fight,
  Whom God Himself elected.
Ask ye His name? 'tis Christ our Lord,
The God of Hosts alone adored,
  Our Champion—none dare brave Him.

Should Hell's whole legions round us press,
  All banded to devour us,
Yet this should work us good success,
  Nor fear e'en then o'erpower us;
Though this world's Prince look fierce and bold,
It matters not, his doom is told,
  A single word can foil him.

Henry J. Buckoll, 1842,
from the German of Martin Luther, 1529.

268

P. M.

TO Thee, O loving Saviour, our spirits turn for
  rest,
Our peace is in Thy favour, our hearts in Thee are
  blest.
Though all the world deceive us, we know that Thou
  art near,
For Thou wilt never leave us, O Christ, our Saviour
  dear.

In Thee our trust abideth, on Thee our hopes rely,
O Thou whose love provideth for all beneath the
  sky.
Our joy is in Thy beauty of holiness divine,
Our comfort in the duty that binds our life in Thine.

O for true hearts to love Thee more dearly as we
  ought,
And nothing place above Thee in word or deed or
  thought.
O for that choicest blessing of living in Thy love,
And thus on earth possessing the peace of heaven
  above.

John S. B. Monsell, 1863.

269

S. M.

BLEST be Thy love, dear Lord,
That taught us this sweet way,
Only to love Thee for Thyself,
And for that love obey.

O Thou, our souls' chief hope,
We to Thy mercy fly ;
Whate'er we are, Thou canst protect,
Whate'er we need, supply.

Whether we sleep or wake,
To Thee we both resign ;
By night we see, as well as day,
If Thy light on us shine.

Whether we live or die,
Both we submit to Thee ;
In death we live, as well as life,
If Thine in death we be.

John Austin, 1668.

270

Four 6's

LORD, Thy word abideth,
And our footsteps guideth ;
Who its truth believeth
Light and joy receiveth.

When our foes are near us,
Then Thy word doth cheer us,
Word of consolation,
Message of salvation.

When the storms are o'er us,
And dark clouds before us,
Then its light directeth,
And our way protecteth.

Who can tell the pleasure,
Who recount the treasure
By Thy word imparted
To the simple-hearted ?

Word of mercy, giving
Succour to the living ;
Word of life, supplying
Comfort to the dying !

Oh, that we discerning
Its most holy learning,
Lord, may love and fear Thee,
Evermore be near Thee.

Sir Henry W. Baker, 1861.

271

C. M.

GOD moves in a mysterious way
  His wonders to perform :
He plants His footsteps in the sea,
  And rides upon the storm.

Deep in unfathomable mines
  Of never-failing skill
He treasures up His bright designs,
  And works His sovereign will.

Ye fearful saints, fresh courage take !
  The clouds ye so much dread
Are big with mercy, and shall break
  In blessings on your head.

Judge not the Lord by feeble sense,
  But trust Him for His grace ;
Behind a frowning providence
  He hides a smiling face.

Blind unbelief is sure to err,
  And scan His work in vain ;
God is His own interpreter,
  And He will make it plain.

William Cowper, 1779.

T

272

D. 8. 8. 6.

O LORD, how happy should we be
If we could cast our care on Thee:
　　If we from self could rest ;
And feel at heart that One above,
In perfect wisdom, perfect love,
　　Is working for the best !

Could we but kneel and cast our load
E'en while we pray, upon our God,
　　Then rise with lightened cheer ;
Sure that the Father, who is nigh
To still the famished raven's cry,
　　Will hear in that we fear.

We cannot trust Him as we should,
So chafes weak nature's restless mood
　　To cast its peace away ;
Yet birds and flowers around us preach ;
All, all the present evil teach
　　Sufficient for the day.

Lord, make these faithless hearts of ours
Such lesson learn from birds and flowers :
　　Make them from self to cease,
Leave all things to a Father's will,
And taste, before Him lying still,
　　E'en in affliction, peace.

Joseph Austice, 1836.

273

8. 8. 8. 4.

JESU, my Saviour, look on me,
For I am weary and opprest ;
I come to cast myself on Thee :
    Thou art my Rest.

Look down on me, for I am weak,
I feel the toilsome journey's length,
Thine aid omnipotent I seek :
    Thou art my Strength.

I am bewildered on my way ;
Dark and tempestuous is the night ;
Oh, send Thou forth some cheering ray :
    Thou art my Light.

When Satan flings his fiery darts,
I look to Thee—my terrors cease ;
Thy Cross a hiding-place imparts :
    Thou art my Peace.

Standing alone on Jordan's brink,
In that tremendous latest strife,
Thou wilt not suffer me to sink :
    Thou art my Life.

Thou wilt my every want supply,
E'en to the end, whate'er befall ;
Through life, in death, eternally,
    Thou art my All.

John R. Macduff, 1853.

274

C. M.

THOU art the Way ! by Thee alone
  From sin and death we flee ;
And he who would the Father seek,
  Must seek Him, Lord, by Thee.

Thou art the Truth ! Thy word alone
  True wisdom can impart ;
Thou only canst inform the mind,
  And purify the heart.

Thou art the Life ! the rending tomb
  Proclaims Thy conquering arm ;
And those who put their trust in Thee
  Nor death nor hell shall harm.

Thou art the Way, the Truth, the Life !
  Grant us that Way to know,
That Truth to keep, that Life to win
  Whence joys eternal flow.

Bishop Doane, 1824.

275

Three 8's.

WHY should I fear the darkest hour,
Or tremble at the tempter's power?
Jesus vouchsafes to be my tower.

When earthly comforts fade and die,
Though others weep, yet why should I?
Jesus still lives, and still is nigh.

I know not what may soon betide,
Or how my wants shall be supplied ;
But Jesus knows, and will provide.

Though sin would fill me with distress,
The throne of grace I dare address,
For Jesus is my righteousness.

Against me earth and hell combine :
But on my side is power divine ;
Jesus is all, and He is mine.

John Newton, 1779.

276

D. C. M.

WHY pour'st thou forth thine anxious plaint,
  Despairing of relief,
As if the Lord o'erlooked thy cause,
  And did not heed thy grief?
Hast thou not known, hast thou not heard,
  That firm remains on high
The everlasting throne of Him
  Who formed the earth and sky?

Art thou afraid His power should fail,
  When comes the evil day?
And can an all-creating arm
  Grow weary, or delay?
Supreme in wisdom as in power,
  The Rock of Ages stands ;
Though Him thou canst not see, nor trace
  The working of His hands.

He gives the conquest to the weak,
  Supports the fainting heart ;
And courage in the evil hour
  His heavenly aids impart.
Mere human power shall fast decay,
  And youthful vigour cease ;
But they who wait upon the Lord
  In strength shall still increase.

They with unwearied feet shall tread
  The path of life divine ;
With growing ardour onward move,
  With growing brightness shine.
On eagle's wings they mount, they soar,
  Their wings are faith and love ;
Till, past the cloudy regions here,
  They rise to heaven above.

Varied by William Cameron, 1770,
  from Isaac Watts, 1709.

277

L. M.

BESET with snares on every hand,
In life's uncertain path we stand ;
Saviour divine ! diffuse Thy light,
And guide our doubtful footsteps right.

Engage each weak and erring heart
Early to choose the better part ;
To yield the trifles of a day
For joys that never fade away.

Then should the wildest storms arise,
And tempests mingle earth and skies,
No fatal shipwreck shall we fear,
But all our treasure with us bear.

If Thou, our Saviour, still art nigh,
Cheerful we live, and cheerful die ;
Secure, when human comforts flee,
To find eternal joys in Thee.

Philip Doddridge, 1755.

278

(PSALM XXIII.)

Six 8's.

THE Lord my pasture shall prepare,
And feed me with a shepherd's care ;
His presence shall my wants supply,
And guard me with a watchful eye ;
My noonday walks He shall attend,
And all my midnight hours defend.

When in the sultry glebe I faint,
Or on the thirsty mountain pant,
To fertile vales and dewy meads
My weary wandering steps He leads ;
Where peaceful rivers, soft and slow,
Amid the verdant landscape flow.

Though in a bare and rugged way
Through devious, lonely wilds I stray,
His bounty shall my pains beguile ;
The barren wilderness shall smile,
With sudden green and herbage crowned,
And streams shall murmur all around.

Though in the paths of death I tread,
With gloomy horrors overspread,
My steadfast heart shall fear no ill,
For Thou, O Lord, art with me still !
Thy friendly crook shall give me aid,
And guide me through the dreadful shade.

Joseph Addison, 1712.

279

(PSALM XXIII.)

8. 7. 8. 7.

THE King of love my Shepherd is,
 Whose goodness faileth never ;
I nothing lack if I am His
 And He is mine for ever.

Where streams of living water flow,
 My ransomed soul He leadeth,
And where the verdant pastures grow
 With food celestial feedeth.

Perverse and foolish oft I strayed,
 But yet in love He sought me,
And on His shoulder gently laid,
 And home rejoicing brought me.

In death's dark vale I fear no ill,
 With Thee, dear Lord, beside me ;
Thy rod and staff my comfort still,
 Thy cross before to guide me.

Thou spread'st a table in my sight ;
 Thy unction grace bestoweth ;
And oh, what transport of delight
 From Thy pure chalice floweth !

And so through all the length of days
 Thy goodness faileth never :
Good Shepherd, may I sing Thy praise
 Within Thy house for ever.

Sir Henry W. Baker, 1868.

280

(Psalm XXXVII.)

S. M.

COMMIT thou all thy griefs
And ways into His hands,
To His sure truth and tender care
Who earth and heaven commands.

Thou on the Lord rely ;
So safe shalt thou go on ;
Fix on His work thy steadfast eye,
So shall thy work be done.

Thy everlasting truth,
Father ! Thy ceaseless love,
Sees all Thy children's wants, and knows
What best for each will prove.

Give to the winds thy fears,
Hope, and be undismayed ;
God hears thy sighs, and counts thy tears,
God shall lift up thy head.

Leave to His sovereign sway
To choose and to command ;
So shalt thou wondering own, His way
How wise, how strong His hand !

Let us in life, in death,
Thy steadfast truth declare,
And publish with our latest breath
Thy love and guardian care.

John Wesley, 1739,
from the German of Paul Gerhardt, 1653.

281

(PSALM XXXVII.)

S. M.

PUT thou thy trust in God,
In duty's path go on ;
Walk in His strength with faith and hope,
So shall thy work be done.

Commit thy ways to Him,
Thy works into His hands,
And rest on His unchanging word,
Who heaven and earth commands.

Though years on years roll on,
His covenant shall endure ;
Though clouds and darkness hide His path,
The promised grace is sure.

Through waves and clouds and storms
His power will clear thy way :
In God's own time the darkest night
Will end in brightest day.

John Wesley, 1743,
from the German of Paul Gerhardt, 1653.

282

(Psalm XLII.)

C. M.

AS pants the hart for cooling streams
  When heated in the chase,
So longs my soul, O God, for Thee,
  And Thy refreshing grace.

For Thee, my God, the living God,
  My thirsty soul doth pine :
Oh, when shall I behold Thy face,
  Thou Majesty divine ?

Why restless, why cast down, my soul?
  Hope still, and thou shalt sing
The praise of Him Who is thy God,
  Thy health's eternal spring.

To Father, Son and Holy Ghost,
  The God whom we adore,
Be glory, as it was, is now,
  And shall be evermore.

Tate and Brady, 1696.

283

(Psalm LXXXVII.)

D. 8. 7. 8. 7.

GLORIOUS things of thee are spoken,
 Zion, city of our God ;
He, whose word cannot be broken,
 Formed thee for His own abode ;
On the Rock of Ages founded,
 What can shake thy sure repose ?
With Salvation's walls surrounded,
 Thou may'st smile at all thy foes.

Though the world esteem thee lowly,
 Though they pass thy ramparts by,
Yet the Lord whose name is holy,
 He who fills Eternity,
He whom not the heaven containeth,
 Not the high and holy place,
Still within thy walls remaineth,
 Still upholds thee with His grace.

See the streams of living waters,
 Springing from eternal love,
Still supply thy sons and daughters,
 And all pain and thirst remove :
Heed not then reproach and scorning ;
 Fear not threats nor danger near :
Soon shall rise a brighter morning,
 When thy Lord shall reappear.

John Newton, 1779.

284

(Psalm XCI.)

D. 8. 7. 8. 7.

CALL Jehovah thy salvation ;
  Rest beneath the Almighty's shade ;
In His sacred habitation
  Dwell, nor ever be afraid.
There no tumult can alarm thee,
  Thou shalt dread no hidden snare ;
Guile nor violence can harm thee,
  In eternal safeguard there.

From the sword at noonday wasting,
  From the noisome pestilence,
In the depth of midnight blasting,
  God will be thy sure defence :
Fear not then the deadly quiver,
  Though a thousand feel the blow ;
Mercy shall thy soul deliver,
  Though ten thousand be laid low.

If with pure and firm affection
  On God's laws be set thy love,
With the wings of His protection
  He will shield thee from above :
Thou shalt call when griefs oppress thee,
  He will hearken, He will save ;
Here with special favour bless thee,
  Give thee life beyond the grave.

James Montgomery, 1822.

285

(PSALM XC.)

C. M.

O GOD, our help in ages past.
 Our hope for years to come,
Our shelter from the stormy blast,
 And our eternal home !

Beneath the shadow of Thy throne
 Thy saints have dwelt secure ;
Sufficient is Thine arm alone
 And our defence is sure.

Before the hills in order stood,
 Or earth received her frame,
From everlasting Thou art God,
 To endless years the same.

A thousand ages in Thy sight
 Are like an evening gone,
Short as the watch that ends the night
 Before the rising sun.

Time, like an ever-rolling stream,
 Bears all its sons away ;
They fly forgotten, as a dream
 Dies at the opening day.

O God, our help in ages past,
 Our hope for years to come,
Be Thou our guide while life shall last,
 And our eternal home !

Isaac Watts, 1719.

286

(PSALM CV.) D. C. M.

O PRAISE our great and gracious Lord,
　And call upon His name ;
To strains of joy tune every chord,
　His mighty acts proclaim ;
Tell how He led His chosen race
　To Canaan's promised land ;
Tell how His covenant of grace
　Unchanged shall ever stand.

He gave the shadowing cloud by day,
　The moving fire by.night ;
To guide His Israel on their way,
　He made their darkness light :
And have we not a sure retreat,
　A Saviour ever nigh,
The same clear light to guide our feet,
　The Dayspring from on high?

We, too, have manna from above,
　The Bread that came from heaven ;
To us the same kind hand of love
　Has living waters given :
A Rock have we, from whence the spring
　In rich abundance flows ;
That Rock is Christ, our Priest, our King,
　Who life and health bestows.

Oh, may we prize this blessed Food,
　And trust our heavenly Guide ;
So shall we find death's fearful flood
　Serene as Jordan's tide :
And safely reach that happy shore,
　The land of peace and rest,
Where angels worship and adore
　In God's own presence blest.

Harriet Auber, 1829.

287

(Psalm CXXI.)

C. M.

FROM Sion's hill my help descends ;
  To God I lift mine eyes ;
My strength on Him alone depends
  Who formed the earth and skies.

He, ever watchful, ever nigh,
  Forbids my foot to slide ;
Nor sleep, nor slumber, seals the eye
  Of Israel's guard and guide.

He, on my side, arrayed in might,
  His shield shall o'er me spread ;
Nor sun by day, nor moon by night,
  Shall hurt my favoured head.

Safe shall I go, and safe return,
  While He my life defends,
Whose eyes my every step discern,
  Whose mercy never ends.

Edward Osler, 1836.

288

6. 4. 6. 4. 6. 6. 4.

NEARER my God, to Thee,
  Nearer to Thee !
E'en though it be a cross
  That raiseth me,
Still all my song shall be,
Nearer, my God, to Thee,
  Nearer to Thee !

Though like the wanderer,
  The sun gone down,
Darkness comes over me,
  My rest a stone ;
Yet in my dreams I'd be
Nearer, my God, to Thee,
  Nearer to Thee.

There let my way appear
  Steps unto heaven,
All that Thou sendest me
  In mercy given ;
Angels to beckon me
Nearer, my God, to Thee,
  Nearer to Thee.

Then with my waking thoughts
  Bright with Thy praise,
Out of my stony griefs
  Bethel I'll raise ;
So by my woes to be
Nearer, my God, to Thee,
  Nearer to Thee.

Sarah F. Adams, 1841.

289

Four 6's.

THY way, not mine, O Lord,
　However dark it be :
Lead me by Thine own hand,
　Choose out the path for me.

Smooth let it be or rough,
　It will be still the best :
Winding or straight, it leads
　Right onward to Thy rest.

I dare not choose my lot ;
　I would not if I might ;
Choose Thou for me, my God,
　So shall I walk aright.

The kingdom that I seek
　Is Thine ; so let the way
That leads to it be Thine ;
　Else I must surely stray.

Take Thou my cup, and it
　With joy or sorrow fill,
As best to Thee may seem ;
　Choose Thou my good and ill.

Choose Thou for me my friends,
　My sickness or my health ;
Choose Thou my cares for me,
　My poverty or wealth.

Not mine, not mine the choice,
　In things or great or small ;
Be Thou my guide, my strength,
　My wisdom, and my all !

Horatius Bonar, 1856.

290

8. 8. 8. 4.

MY God, my Father, while I stray
Far from my home, on life's rough way,
Oh, teach me from my heart to say,
    Thy will be done !

Though dark my path and sad my lot,
Let me be still, and murmur not,
Or breathe the prayer divinely taught,
    Thy will be done !

If Thou shouldst call me to resign
What most I prize, it ne'er was mine ;
I only yield Thee what was Thine—
    Thy will be done !

Let but my fainting heart be blest
With Thy sweet Spirit for its guest,
My God to Thee I leave the rest—
    Thy will be done !

Renew my will from day to day ;
Blend it with Thine, and take away
All that now makes it hard to say,
    Thy will be done !

Then, when on earth I breathe no more
The prayer, oft mixed with tears before,
I'll sing upon a happier shore,
    Thy will be done !

Charlotte Elliott, 1834.

291

10. 4. 10. 4. 10. 10.

LEAD, kindly Light, amid the encircling gloom,
    Lead Thou me on ;
The night is dark, and I am far from home,
    Lead Thou me on.
Keep Thou my feet—I do not ask to see
The distant scene—one step enough for me.

I was not ever thus, nor prayed that Thou
    Shouldst lead me on ;
I loved to choose and see my path—but now
    Lead Thou me on.
I loved the garish day ; and, spite of fears,
Pride ruled my will : remember not past years.

So long Thy power hath blest me, sure it still
    Will lead me on
O'er moor and fen, o'er crag and torrent, till
    The night is gone,
And with the morn those angel faces smile,
Which I have loved long since, and lost a while.

John H. Newman, 1833.

292

Six 8's.

WE saw Thee not, when Thou didst tread,
  O Saviour, this our sinful earth ;
Nor heard Thy voice restore the dead,
  And wake them to a second birth :
But we believe that Thou didst come,
And quit for us Thy glorious home.

We were not with the faithful few
  Who stood Thy bitter cross around.
Nor heard the prayer for those who slew,
  Nor felt the earthquake rock the ground ;
We saw no spear-wound pierce Thy side :
Yet we believe that Thou hast died.

No angel's message met our ear
  On that first glorious Easter Day,
"The Lord is risen, He is not here,
  Come see the place where Jesus lay !"
But we believe that Thou didst quell
The banded powers of Death and Hell.

We saw Thee not return on high,—
  And now, our longing sight to bless,
No ray of glory from the sky
  Shines down upon our wilderness :
Yet we believe that Thou art there,
And seek Thee, Lord, in praise and prayer.

John H. Gurney, 1851.

293

C. M.

WE walk by faith and not by sight ;
  No gracious words we hear
From Him who spake as man ne'er spake,
  But we believe Him near.

We may not touch His hands and side,
  Nor follow where He trod ;
But in His promise we rejoice,
  And cry, " My Lord and God ! "

Help then, O Lord, our unbelief ;
  And may our faith abound,
To call on Thee when Thou art near,
  And seek where Thou art found :

That, when our life of faith is done,
  In realms of clearer light
We may behold Thee as Thou art,
  With full and endless sight.

Henry Alford, 1845.

294

Four 7's.

OFT in danger, oft in woe,
Onward, Christians, onward go !
Fight the fight, maintain the strife,
Strengthened with the bread of life.

Onward, Christians, onward go !
Join the war, and face the foe ;
Will ye flee in danger's hour ?
Know ye not your Captain's power ?

Let your drooping hearts be glad ;
March in heavenly armour clad ;
Fight, nor think the battle long ;
Soon shall victory wake your song.

Let not sorrow dim your eye ;
Soon shall every tear be dry ;
Let not fears your course impede ;
Great your strength, if great your need.

Onward, then, to battle move ;
More than conquerors ye shall prove ;
Though opposed by many a foe,
Christian soldiers, onward go !

Fragment by Henry Kirke White, 1806,
completed by Fanny F. Maitland, 1827.

295

D. 6. 5. 6. 5.

SAVIOUR, blessed Saviour,
  Listen whilst we sing,
Hearts and voices raising
  Praises to our King ;
All we have to offer,
  All we hope to be,
Body, soul, and spirit,
  All we yield to Thee.

Great and ever greater
  Are Thy mercies here ;
True and everlasting
  Are the glories there,
Where no pain or sorrow,
  Toil or care, is known,
Where the angel-legions
  Circle round Thy throne.

Clearer still and clearer
  Dawns the light from heaven,
In our sadness bringing
  News of sin forgiven ;
Life has lost its shadows,
  Pure the light within ;
Thou hast shed Thy radiance
  On a world of sin.

Onward, ever onward,
  Journeying o'er the road
Worn by saints before us,
  Journeying on to God ;
Leaving all behind us,
  May we hasten on,
Backward never looking
  Till the prize is won.

Godfrey Thring, 1866

296

JERUSALEM, my happy home,
  Name ever dear to me,
When shall my labours have an end
  In joy, and peace, and thee?

When shall these eyes thy heaven-built walls
  And pearly gates behold?
Thy bulwarks with salvation strong,
  And streets of shining gold?

Why should I shrink from pain and woe,
  Or feel at death dismay,
With Canaan's goodly land in view,
  And realms of endless day?

Apostles, martyrs, prophets there
  Around my Saviour stand;
And all I love in Christ below
  Shall join the glorious band.

Jerusalem, my happy home,
  My soul still pants for thee!
Then shall my labours have an end,
  When I thy joys shall see.

F. B. P., 1616,
from a Latin hymn of the 8th century.

297

7. 6. 7. 6.

BRIEF life is here our portion,
   Brief sorrow, short-lived care :
The life that knows no ending,
   The tearless life, is there.

Oh, happy retribution,
   Short toil, eternal rest !
For mortals and for sinners
   A mansion with the blest.

And now we fight the battle,
   But then shall wear the crown
Of full and everlasting
   And passionless renown :

The God whom now we trust in
   Shall then be seen and known ;
And they who see and know Him
   Shall have Him for their own.

The morning shall awaken,
   The shadows shall decay,
And each true-hearted servant
   Shall shine as doth the day.

There God, our King and Portion,
   In fulness of His grace,
Shall we behold for ever,
   And worship face to face.

John M. Neale, 1858,
from the Latin of Bernard of Cluny, ✠ 1156.

298

7. 6. 7. 6.

JERUSALEM the Golden,
  With milk and honey blest,
Beneath thy contemplation
  Sink heart and voice opprest.

I know not—oh, I know not
  What joys await us there,
What radiancy of glory,
  What bliss beyond compare !

And when I fain would sing them
  My spirit fails and faints,
And vainly would it image
  The assembly of the saints.

They stand, those halls of Sion,
  Full jubilant with song,
And bright with many an angel
  And many a martyr-throng.

The Prince is ever in them,
  The light is aye serene ;
The pastures of the blessèd
  Are decked in glorious sheen.

And they, beneath their Leader
  Who conquered in the fight,
For ever and for ever
  Are clad in robes of white.

John M. Neale, 1858,
from the Latin of Bernard of Cluny, ✠ 1156.

299

C. M.

THERE is a land of pure delight,
    Where saints immortal reign ;
Infinite day excludes the night,
    And pleasures banish pain.

There everlasting spring abides,
    And never-withering flowers :
Death, like a narrow sea, divides
    This heavenly land from ours.

Sweet fields beyond the swelling flood
    Stand dressed in living green :
So to the Jews old Canaan stood,
    While Jordan rolled between.

But timorous mortals start and shrink
    To cross this narrow sea,
And linger shivering on the brink,
    And fear to launch away.

Oh, could we make our doubts remove,
    These gloomy doubts that rise,
And see the Canaan that we love
    With unbeclouded eyes ;

Could we but climb where Moses stood,
    And view the landscape o'er,
Not Jordan's stream, nor death's cold flood,
    Should fright us from the shore !

Isaac Watts, 1709.

300

Eight 6's

THERE is a blessèd home
  Beyond this land of woe,
Where trials never come,
  Nor tears of sorrow flow ;
Where faith is lost in sight,
  And patient hope is crowned,
And everlasting light
  Its glory throws around.

There is a land of peace,
  Good angels know it well ;
Glad songs that never cease
  Within its portals swell ;
Around its glorious throne
  Ten thousand saints adore
Christ, with the Father One
  And Spirit, evermore.

Look up, ye saints of God,
  Nor fear to tread below
The path your Saviour trod
  Of daily toil and woe ;
Wait but a little while
  In uncomplaining love,
His own most gracious smile
  Shall welcome you above.

Sir Henry W. Baker, 1861.

301

Four 7's.

CHILDREN of the Heavenly King,
As ye journey, sweetly sing ;
Sing your Saviour's worthy praise,
Glorious in His works and ways.

We are travelling home to God,
In the way the Fathers trod ;
They are happy now, and we
Soon their happiness shall see.

Fear not, brethren ; joyful stand
On the borders of your land ;
Jesus Christ, your Father's Son,
Bids you undismayed go on.

Lord, obediently we go,
Gladly leaving all below ;
Only Thou our Leader be,
And we still will follow Thee

John Cennick, 1742.

302

D. S. M.

"FOR ever with the Lord!"
Amen, so let it be;
Life from the dead is in that word,
'Tis immortality.
Here in the body pent,
Absent from Him I roam,
Yet nightly pitch my moving tent
A day's march nearer home.

My Father's house on high,
Home of my soul, how near
At times to faith's foreseeing eye
Thy golden gates appear!
Ah, then my spirit faints
To reach the land I love,
The bright inheritance of saints,
Jerusalem above.

"For ever with the Lord!"
Father, if 'tis Thy will,
The promise of that faithful word
Even here to me fulfil.
Be Thou at my right hand,
Then can I never fail;
Uphold Thou me, and I shall stand.
Fight, and I must prevail.

So when my latest breath
Shall rend the veil in twain,
By death I shall escape from death,
And life eternal gain.
Knowing as I am known,
How shall I love that word,
And oft repeat before the throne,
"For ever with the Lord!"

James Montgomery, 1853.

303

6. 6. 8. 6. 4. 7.

FROM Egypt's bondage come,
  Where death and darkness reign,
We seek a new, a better home,
  Where we our rest shall gain.
     Hallelujah !
We are on our way to God.

There sin and sorrow cease,
  And every conflict's o'er ;
There we shall dwell in endless peace,
  And never hunger more.
     Hallelujah !
We are on our way to God.

There in celestial strains
  Enraptured myriads sing ;
There love in every bosom reigns,
  For God Himself is King.
     Hallelujah !
We are on our way to God.

We soon shall join the throng,
  Their pleasures we shall share,
And sing the everlasting song
  With all the ransomed there.
     Hallelujah !
Bring us safe to Thee, O God !

Thomas Kelly, 1806.

304

(PSALM LXXXIV.)   Eight 7's.

PLEASANT are Thy courts above
In the land of light and love ;
Pleasant are Thy courts below
In this land of sin and woe :
Oh, my spirit longs and faints
For the converse of Thy saints,
For the brightness of Thy face,
For Thy fulness, God of grace.

Happy birds that sing and fly
Round Thy altars, O most High ;
Happier souls that find a rest
In a heavenly Father's breast ;
Like the wandering dove that found
No repose on earth around,
They can to their ark repair,
And enjoy it ever there.

Happy souls, their praises flow
Even in this vale of woe ;
Waters in the deserts rise,
Manna feeds them from the skies ;
On they go from strength to strength,
Till they reach Thy throne at length,
At Thy feet adoring fall,
Who hast led them safe through all.

Lord, be mine this prize to win,
Guide me through a world of sin,
Keep me by Thy saving grace,
Give me at Thy side a place ;
Sun and Shield alike Thou art,
Guide and guard my erring heart ;
Grace and glory flow from Thee ;
Shower, O shower them, Lord, on me.

Henry F. Lyte, 1834.

305

(PSALM XXVI. 8.)

Four 6's.

WE love the place, O Lord,
  Wherein Thine honour dwells;
The joy of Thine abode
  All earthly joy excels.

It is the house of prayer,
  Wherein Thy servants meet;
And Thou, O Lord, art there
  Thy chosen flock to greet.

We love Thine altar, Lord;
  Oh, what on earth so dear?
For there, in faith adored,
  We find Thy presence near.

We love the word of life,
  The word that tells of peace,
Of comfort in the strife,
  And joys that never cease.

We love to sing below
  For mercies freely given;
But, oh, we long to know
  The triumph-song of heaven.

Lord Jesus, give us grace
  On earth to love Thee more,
In heaven to see Thy face,
  And with Thy saints adore.

*First three verses by William Bullock, 1854,
last three by Sir Henry W. Baker, 1861.*

306

8. 5. 8. 3.

ART thou weary, art thou languid,
    Art thou sore distrest?
" Come to Me," saith One, "and coming
        Be at rest."

Hath He marks to lead me to Him,
    If He be my guide?
" In His feet and hands are wound-prints,
        And His side."

Hath He diadem as monarch
    That His brow adorns?
" Yea, a crown, in very surety,
        But of thorns."

If I find Him, if I follow,
    What His guerdon here?
" Many a sorrow, many a labour,
        Many a tear."

If I still hold closely to Him,
    What hath He at last?
" Sorrow vanquished, labour ended,
        Jordan past."

If I ask Him to receive me,
    Will He say me nay?
" Not till earth and not till heaven
        Pass away."

Finding, following, keeping, struggling,
    Is He sure to bless?
" Angels, martyrs, prophets, virgins,
        Answer, Yes."

John M. Neale, 1862,
from the Greek of S. Stephen the Sabaite, ✠ 794.

307

8. 6. 8. 6. 4. 9.

WHO shall ascend to the holy place,
    And stand on the holy hill?
Who shall the boundless realms of space
    With shouts of rapture thrill?
        Hallelujah!
For the Lord God Omnipotent reigneth!

The servants of the Lord are they,
    The pure in heart and hand,
For whom the eternal bars give way,
    The eternal gates expand!
        Hallelujah!
For the Lord God Omnipotent reigneth!

Not to the noble, not to the strong,
    To the wealthy, or the wise,
Is given a part in that angel-song,
    That music of the skies;
        Hallelujah!
For the Lord God Omnipotent reigneth!

But those who in humble and holy fear,
    With child-like faith and love,
Have served the Lord as their Master here,
    Shall praise the Lord above.
        Hallelujah!
For the Lord God Omnipotent reigneth!

And chiefly those who in youth to Him
    Their morn of life have given,
With Cherubim and Seraphim,
    And all the host of heaven—
        Hallelujah!
For the Lord God Omnipotent reigneth!

—Shall stand in robes of purest white,
    And to the Lamb shall raise
The song that rests not day and night,
    The eternity of praise.
        Hallelujah!
For the Lord God Omnipotent reigneth!

Thomas E. Hankinson, 1840.

· 308 ·

Six 6's.

O THOU not made with hands,
Not throned above the skies,
Nor walled with shining walls,
Nor framed with stones of price,
  More bright than gold or gem,
  God's own Jerusalem !

Where'er the gentle heart
Finds courage from above ;
Where'er the heart forsook
Warms with the breath of love ;
  Where faith bids fear depart,
  City of God, Thou art !

Thou art where'er the proud
In humbleness melts down ;
Where self itself yields up ;
Where martyrs win their crown ;
  Where faithful souls possess
  Themselves in perfect peace.

Where in life's common ways
With cheerful feet we go ;
Where in His steps we tread
Who trod the way of woe ;
  Where He is in the heart,
  City of God, thou art !

Not throned above the skies,
Nor golden-walled afar,
But where Christ's two or three
In His name gathered are,
  Be in the midst of them,
  God's own Jerusalem !

Francis T. Palgrave, 1867.

ANTHEMS AND INTROITS.

I

SLEEPERS awake! a voice is calling, it is the watchman on the walls; thou city of Jerusalem! For lo! the Bridegroom comes! Arise and take your lamps! Hallelujah! Awake! His kingdom is at hand! Go forth to meet your Lord!

Philip Nicolai (*Mendelssohn*).

2

O GOD, who by the leading of a star didst manifest Thy only-begotten Son to the Gentiles; mercifully grant, that we, which know Thee now by faith, may after this life have the fruition of Thy glorious Godhead; through Jesus Christ our Lord. Amen.

Collect for the Epiphany (*W. S. Bambridge*).

3

ENTER not into judgment with Thy servant, O Lord, for in Thy sight shall no man living be justified.

Psalm cxliii. 2 (*Attwood*).

4

INCLINE Thine ear to me, O Lord, make haste to deliver me ; O save me for Thy mercies' sake.

(Himmel.)

5

LORD, for Thy tender mercies' sake, lay not our sins to our charge, but forgive that is past, and give us grace to amend our sinful lives, to decline from sin, and incline to virtue : that we may walk with a perfect heart before Thee now and evermore.

(Farrant.)

6

LIKE as the hart desireth the water-brooks, so longeth my soul after Thee, O God. Why art thou so full of heaviness, O my soul ; and why art thou so disquieted within me?

O put thy trust in God.

Psalm xlii. 1, 6, 7 *(Novello)*.

7

CALL to remembrance, O Lord, Thy tender mercies : and Thy loving-kindnesses, which have been ever of old. O remember not the sins and offences of my youth : but according to Thy mercy think Thou upon me, O Lord, for Thy goodness.

Psalm xxv. 5, 6 *(Farrant)*.

8

REND your hearts and not your garments, and turn unto the Lord your God ; for He is gracious and merciful, slow to anger, and of great kindness, and repenteth Him of the evil.

Joel ii. 13.

9

NOW, saith the Lord, turn ye ever to me with all your heart, and with fasting, and with weeping, and with mourning ;

And rend your hearts and not your garments, and turn unto the Lord your God ; for He is gracious and merciful, slow to anger, and of great kindness, and repenteth Him of the evil.

Joel ii. 12, 13 (*Macfarren*).

10

TURN Thy face from my sins, and put out all my misdeeds. Make me a clean heart, O God ! and renew a right spirit within me. Cast me not away from Thy presence, and take not Thy Holy Spirit from me.

Psalm li. 9—11 (*Attwood*).

11

CAST thy burden upon the Lord, and He shall sustain thee ; He never will suffer the righteous to fall ; He is at thy right hand. Thy mercy, Lord, is great, and far above the heavens.

Let none be made ashamed that wait upon Thee.

(*Mendelssohn*).

12

FOR our offences Jesus took upon Him humility, and unto death even upon the cross became He obedient; God therefore Him hath exalted, and on Him a name hath bestowed high above every mortal name. Amen. (*Mendelssohn.*)

13

CHRIST our passover is sacrificed for us : therefore let us keep the feast, not with the old leaven, neither with the leaven of malice and wickedness ; but with the unleavened bread of sincerity and truth.   1 Cor. v. 7, 8 (*Goss*).

14

FOR if we believe that Jesus died and rose again, even so them also which sleep in Jesus will God bring with Him. Amen.

1 Thess. iv. 14 (*Macfarren*).

15

O HOLY GHOST, into our minds
   Send down Thy heavenly light,
Kindle our hearts with fervent zeal
   To serve God day and night.
Thou art the very Comforter
   In grief and all distress,
The heavenly gift of God most high,
   No tongue can it express.
Such measure of Thy powerful grace
   Grant to us, Lord, we pray,
That Thou mayst be our Comforter
   At the last awful day.

(*Macfarren.*)

16

GOD is a Spirit: and they that worship Him must worship Him in spirit and in truth.

John iv. 24 (*Sterndale Bennett*).

17

O PRAISE God in His holiness: praise Him in the firmament of His power. Praise Him in His noble acts: praise Him according to His excellent greatness. Praise Him in the sound of the trumpet: praise Him upon the lute and harp. Praise Him in the cymbals and dances: praise Him upon the strings and pipe.

Praise Him upon the well-tuned cymbals: praise Him upon the loud cymbals. Let everything that hath breath praise the Lord.

Psalm cl. (*Weldon*).

18

NOT unto us, O Lord, not unto us, but unto Thy name give the praise: for Thy loving mercy, and for Thy truth's sake.

Psalm cxv. 1 (*Walmisley*).

19

O LORD, how manifold are Thy works: in wisdom hast Thou made them all, the earth is full of Thy riches. The valleys stand so thick with corn that they laugh and sing.

Psalm civ. 24; lxv. 14 (*Barnby*).

THINE, O Lord, is the greatness, and the power, and the glory, and the victory, and the majesty; for all that is in the heaven and in the earth is Thine; Thine is the kingdom, O Lord, and Thou art exalted as head over all.

1 Chron. xxix. 11 (*Kent*).

21

WE will rejoice in Thy salvation, and triumph in the name of the Lord our God : the Lord perform all thy petitions.

Now know I that the Lord helpeth His Anointed and will hear him from His holy heaven : even with the saving strength of His right hand.

Some put their trust in chariots and some in horses : but we will remember the name of the Lord our God.

Psalm xx. 5—7 (*Croft*).

22

PRAISED be the Lord daily : even the God who helpeth us, and poureth His benefits upon us.

He is our God, even the God of whom cometh salvation : God is the Lord, by whom we escape death.

Psalm lxviii. 19, 20 (*Ebdon*).

23

O HOW amiable are Thy dwellings : Thou Lord
of hosts !

My soul hath a desire and longing to enter into
the courts of the Lord : my heart and my flesh
rejoice in the living God.

Blessed are They that dwell in Thy house : they
will be always praising Thee.

Psalm lxxxiv. 1, 2, 4 (*Richardson*).

24

BREAD of the world, in mercy broken,
  Wine of the soul, in mercy shed ;
By whom the words of life were spoken,
  And in whose death our sins are dead ;

Look on the heart by sorrow broken,
  Look on the tears by sinners shed,
And be Thy feast to us the token
  That by Thy grace our souls are fed.

Bishop Heber.

25

O LORD my God, hear Thou the prayer Thy
servant prayeth : have Thou respect unto his
prayer. Hear Thou in heaven, Thy dwelling-place,
and when Thou hearest, Lord, forgive.

1 Kings viii. 28 (*Malan*).

26

HEAR my prayer, O Lord : give ear to my supplication. In Thy faithfulness answer me, and in Thy righteousness.

Psalm cxliii. 1 (*Winter*).

27

TEACH me, O Lord, the way of Thy statutes : and I shall keep it unto the end.

Give me understanding, and I shall keep Thy law : yea, I shall keep it with my whole heart.

Make me to go in the path of Thy testimonies : for therein is my desire.

Incline my heart unto Thy testimonies : and not to covetousness.

Behold my delight is in Thy commandments : O quicken me in Thy righteousness.

Psalm cxix. 33—36, 40 (*Rogers*).

28

TEACH me Thy way, O Lord, and I will walk in Thy truth : O knit my heart unto Thee, that I may fear Thy name.

Psalm lxxxvi. 11.

29

TEACH me, O Lord, the way of Thy statutes ; and I shall keep it unto the end.

Psalm cxix. 33 (*Attwood*).

30

TO Thee, O Lord, I yield my spirit,
  Who break'st in love this mortal chain !
My life I but from Thee inherit,
  And death becomes my chiefest gain.
In Thee I live, in Thee I die,
Content, for Thou art ever nigh.

George Neumark (Mendelssohn).

31

I HAVE set God alway before me : for He is on my right hand, therefore shall I not fall.

Wherefore my heart was glad, and my glory rejoiced : my flesh also shall rest in hope.

For Thou wilt not leave my soul in hell, neither shalt Thou suffer Thy Holy One to see corruption.

Thou shalt shew me the path of life ; in Thy presence is fulness of joy : and at Thy right hand there is pleasure for evermore.

Psalm xvi. 9—12 (Blake).

32

BLESSED are they that dwell in Thy house : they will be alway praising Thee.

Blessed is the man whose strength is in Thee : in whose heart are Thy ways.

Who going through the vale of misery use it for a well : and the pools are filled with water.

They will go from strength to strength : and unto the God of Gods appeareth every one of them in Zion.

Psalm lxxxiv. 4, 5, 6, 7 (Tours).

33

IN Thee, O Lord, have I put my trust : let me never be put to confusion, deliver me in Thy righteousness.

Bow down Thine ear to me : make haste to deliver me.

And be Thou my strong rock, and house of defence : that Thou mayest save me.

For Thou art my strong rock, and my castle : be Thou also my guide, and lead me for Thy name's sake.

Psalm xxxi. 1, 2, 3, 4 (*Tours*).

34

NOW on the first day of the week, very early, they came to the sepulchre.

And they found the stone rolled away from the sepulchre.

And they entered in, and found not the body of the Lord Jesus.

But now is Christ risen from the dead, and become the first-fruits of them that slept.

For since by man came death, by man came also the resurrection of the dead.

For as in Adam all die, even so in Christ shall all be made alive.

S. Luke xxiv. 1, 2, 3, and 1 Cor. xv. 20, 21, 22 (*Lahee*).

35

HALLELUJAH ! What are these that are arrayed in white robes ? and whence came they ?

These are they which came out of great tribulation, and have washed their robes, and made them white in the blood of the Lamb.

Hallelujah ! Therefore are they before the throne of God, and serve Him day and night in His temple.

They shall hunger no more, neither thirst any more ; neither shall the sun light on them, nor any heat.

For the Lamb which is in the midst of the throne shall feed them, and shall lead them unto living fountains of waters : and God shall wipe away all tears from their eyes.

Rev. vii. 13, 14, 15, 16, 17 (Stainer).

36

GOD save our gracious Queen,
Long live our noble Queen !
    God save the Queen :
Send her victorious,
Happy and glorious,
Long to reign over us,
    God save the Queen.

Thy choicest gifts in store
On her be pleased to pour ;
    Long may she reign :
May she defend our laws,
And ever give us cause
To sing with heart and voice,
    God save the Queen !

Circa. 1606.

Y

APPENDIX I. AND

APPENDIX I.

I

S. M.

A VOICE by Jordan's shore
A summons stern and clear:
Repent ! Be just, and sin no more !
God's judgment draweth near !

A voice by Galilee,
A holier voice I hear :
Love God ! thy neighbour love ! for see,
God's mercy draweth near !

O voice of Duty, still
Speak forth ; I hear with awe :
In thee I own the sovereign will.
Obey the sovereign law.

Thou higher voice of Love,
Yet speak Thy word in me ;
Through duty let me upward move
To thy pure liberty !

Samuel Johnson (1709 — 1784).

D. 8. 7. 8. 7.

ALLELUIA! Alleluia! hearts and voices heaven-
     ward raise ;
Sing to God a hymn of gladness, sing to God a
     hymn of praise :
He, who on the cross a victim for the world's
     salvation bled,
Jesus Christ, the King of glory, now is risen from
     the dead.

Christ is risen, Christ the firstfruits of the holy
     harvest-field,
Which shall all its full abundance at His second
     coming yield :
Then the golden ears of harvest shall their heads
     before Him wave,
Ripened by His glorious sunshine from the furrows
     of the grave.

Jesu, we in Thee are risen ! Shed on us Thy
     quickening grace,
Rain and dew and gleams of glory from the bright-
     ness of Thy face :
That with hearts in heaven dwelling, we on earth
     may fruitful be,
And by angel-hands be gathered safe for evermore
     with Thee.

                    Bishop Chr. Wordsworth (1807-1885).

3

D. 7. 6. 7. 6.

ALL glory, laud, and honour,
   To Thee, Redeemer, King !
To whom the lips of children
   Made sweet Hosannas ring.

Thou art the King of Israel,
   Thou David's royal Son,
Who in the Lord's Name comest,
   The King and Blessèd One.
              All glory, etc.

The company of angels
   Are praising Thee on high,
And mortal men, and all things
   Created, make reply.
              All glory, etc.

The people of the Hebrews
   With palms before Thee went ;
Our praise and prayer and anthems
   Before Thee we present.
              All glory, etc.

To Thee before Thy Passion
   They sang their hymns of praise ;
To Thee now high exalted
   Our melody we raise.
              All glory, etc.

Thou didst accept their praises ;
   Accept the prayers we bring,
Who in all good delightest,
   Thou good and gracious King.
              All glory, etc.

J. M. Neale,
from S. Theodulphus of Orleans (750-821).

4

ALL is over ;—in the tomb
Sleeps He, 'mid its silent gloom,
Till the dawn of Easter come.

All is over ; fought the fight ;
Heaviness is for a night,
Joy comes with the morning light.

Leave we in the grave with Him
Sins that shame and doubts that dim,
If our souls would rise with Him.

Glory to the Lord, who gave
His pure Body to the grave,
Us from sin and death to save.

W. S. Raymond (1832-1863).

5   8. 5. 8. 5. 8. 4. 3.

ANGEL voices ever singing
  Round Thy throne of light,
Angel harps for ever ringing
  Rest not day nor night :
Thousands only live to bless Thee,
      And confess Thee
        Lord of might !

Thou who art beyond the farthest
  Mortal eye can scan,
Can it be that Thou regardest
  Songs of sinful man ?
Can we know that Thou art near us,
      And wilt hear us ?
        Yea ! we can !

Yea, we know that Thou rejoicest
  O'er each work of Thine ;
Thou didst ears, and hands, and voices,
  For Thy praise design,
Craftsman's art and music's measure
      For Thy pleasure
        All combine.

In Thy house, great God, we offer
  Of Thine own to Thee ;
And for Thine acceptance proffer
  All unworthily
Hearts and minds and hands and voices
      In our choicest
        Psalmody.

Honour, glory, might and merit,
  Thine shall ever be,
Father, Son, and Holy Spirit,
  Blessèd Trinity !
Of the best that Thou hast given,
      Earth and heaven
        Render Thee.
                    Francis Pott.

6

C. M.

" ASK, and ye surely shall receive ; "
    Yea, Lord ! we trust Thy word :
We lift our voice, and we believe
    That we are surely heard.

We ask not anything that earth
    Can give or take away :
Thou, who hast kept us from our birth,
    Wilt guard us day by day.

We ask for light, and love, and strength
    All selfish snares to shun :
We ask that we may ask at length,
    " Thy Will, not ours, be done ! "

We ask that to each separate heart
    Of all our brethren here
Thy one best gift Thou wouldst impart,
    The wisdom of Thy fear.

May young and old conspire to prize,
    And labour to secure,
Whatever things are true, and wise,
    Noble, and just, and pure.

O Thou, by whom we come to God,
    The Life, the Truth, the Way !
The path of prayer Thyself hast trod :
    Lord, teach us how to pray !

              H. M. Butler.
        (last verse from I. Montgomery.)

7

BOUND upon the accursèd tree,
Dread and awful, who is He?
By the sun at noonday pale,
Shivering rocks and rending veil,
Earth that trembles at His doom ;
By the saints who burst their tomb ;
By Eden, promised ere He died
To the felon at His side ;
Lord ! our suppliant knees we bow,
Son of God ! 'tis Thou, 'tis Thou !

Bound upon the accursèd tree,
Sad and dying, who is He?
By the last and bitter cry,
The ghost given up in agony ;
By the lifeless body laid
In the chamber of the dead ;
By the mourners come to weep
Where the bones of Jesus sleep ;
Crucified ! we know Thee now ;
Son of man ! 'tis Thou, 'tis Thou !

Bound upon the accursèd tree,
Dread and awful, who is He?
By the prayer for them that slew,
"Lord ! they know not what they do ! "
By the spoiled and empty grave,
By the souls He died to save,
By the conquest He hath won,
By the saints before His throne,
By the rainbow round His brow,
Son of God ! 'tis Thou, 'tis Thou !

Dean Milman (1791-1868), 1827.

8

4. 10. 10. 10. 4.

COME, labour on !
Who dares stand idle on the harvest plain,
While all around him waves the golden grain ?
And to each servant does the Master say,
    " Go work to-day."

Come, labour on !
Claim the high calling angels cannot share,
To young and old the Gospel-gladness bear ;
Redeem the time ; its hours too swiftly fly,
    The night draws nigh.

Come, labour on !
The enemy is watching night and day,
To sow the tares, to snatch the seed away ;
While we in sleep our duty have forgot,
    He slumbered not.

Come, labour on !
Away with gloomy doubts and faithless fear !
No arm so weak but may do service here ;
By hands the feeblest can our God fulfil
    His righteous will.

Come, labour on !
No time for rest, till glows the western sky,
While the long shadows o'er our pathway lie,
And a glad sound comes with the setting sun—
    " Servants, well done ! "

Come, labour on !
The toil is pleasant, and the harvest sure,
Blessèd are those who to the end endure ;
How full their joy, how deep their rest shall be,
    O Lord, with Thee !

H. L. L.
from " *Thoughts for Thoughtful Hours,*" 1859.

9

D. 7. 6. 7. 6.

" COME unto Me, ye weary,
  " And I will give you rest."
O blessèd voice of Jesus,
  Which comes to hearts opprest !
It tells of benediction,
  Of pardon, grace, and peace,
Of joy that hath no ending,
  Of love which cannot cease.

" Come unto Me, ye wanderers,
  " And I will give you light."
O loving voice of Jesus,
  Which comes to cheer the night !
Our hearts were filled with sadness,
  And we had lost our way ;
But He has brought us gladness
  And songs at break of day.

" Come unto Me, ye fainting,
  " And I will give you life."
O cheering voice of Jesus,
  Which comes to aid our strife !
The foe is stern and eager,
  The fight is fierce and long ;
But He has made us mighty,
  And stronger than the strong.

" And whosoever cometh,
  " I will not cast him out."
O welcome voice of Jesus,
  Which drives away our doubt ;
Which calls us, very sinners,
  Unworthy though we be
Of love so free and boundless,
  To come, dear Lord, to Thee !

                W. Chatterton Dix.

10

Eight 7's.

COME, ye thankful people, come,
Raise the song of Harvest-home !
All is safely gathered in,
Ere the winter-storms begin ;
God, our Maker, doth provide
For our wants to be supplied ;
Come to God's own temple, come ;
Raise the song of Harvest-home !

What is earth but God's own field,
Fruit unto His praise to yield ?
Wheat and tares therein are sown,
Unto joy or sorrow grown ;
Ripening with a wondrous power,
Till the final Harvest-hour ;
Grant, O Lord of Life, that we
Holy grain and pure may be.

For we know that Thou wilt come,
And wilt take Thy people home ;
From Thy field wilt purge away
All that doth offend that day ;
And Thine angels charge at last
In the fire the tares to cast,
But the fruitful ears to store
In Thy garner evermore.

Come then, Lord of mercy, come,
Bid us sing Thy Harvest-home !
Let Thy saints be gathered in,
Free from sorrow, free from sin,
All upon the golden floor
Praising Thee for evermore ;
Come, with thousand angels, come ;
Bid us sing Thy Harvest-home !

Dean Alford (1810—1871).

I I

S. M.

FAIR waved the golden corn,
In Canaan's pleasant land,
When full of joy some shining morn,
Went forth the reaper-band.

To God, so good and great,
Their cheerful thanks they pour ;
Then carry to His temple gate
The choicest of their store.

Like Israel, Lord, we give
Our earliest fruits to Thee,
And pray that, long as we shall live,
We may Thy children be.

Thine is our youthful prime,
And life and all its powers ;
Be with us in our morning time,
And bless our evening hours.

In wisdom let us grow,
As years and strength are given,
That we may serve Thy church below,
And join Thy saints in heaven.

To God, the Father, Son,
And Spirit, ever blest,
The One in Three, and Three in One,
Be endless praise addressed.

J. H. Gurney (1802-1862).

12

D. 7. 5. 7. 5.

FATHER, here we dedicate
  This new year to Thee,
In whatever worldly state
  Thou wilt have us be.
Not from sorrow, pain, or care,
  Freedom dare we claim :
This alone shall be our prayer,
  Glorify Thy name.

Can a child presume to choose
  Where or how to live ?
Can a father's love refuse
  All the best to give ?
More Thou givest every day
  Than the best can claim ;
Nor withholdest aught that may
  Glorify Thy name.

If in mercy Thou wilt spare
  Joys we yet partake ;
If on life, serene and fair,
  Brighter rays may break :
Thee our hearts, while glad they sing,
  Shall in all proclaim ;
And, whate'er the year shall bring,
  Glorify Thy name.

If Thou callest to the Cross,
  And its shadow come,
Turning all our gain to loss,
  Shrouding heart and home ;
Teach us, Lord, how Thy dear Son
  To His glory came ;
In our woe we'll still pray on,
  Glorify Thy name.

Laurence Tuttiett.

13

FATHER, I know that all my life
  Is portioned out for me,
And changes that are sure to come,
  I do not fear to see ;
But ask Thee for a present mind,
  Intent on pleasing Thee.

I ask Thee for a thoughtful love,
  Through constant watching wise,
To meet the glad with joyful smiles,
  And wipe the weeping eyes ;
A heart at leisure from itself,
  To soothe and sympathise.

I ask Thee for the daily strength,
  To none that ask denied,
A mind to blend with outward life,
  While keeping by Thy side :
Content to fill a little space,
  If Thou be glorified.

Briers beset our every path,
  Which call for patient care ;
There is a cross in every lot,
  And earnest need for prayer :
But lowly hearts that lean on Thee,
  Are happy anywhere.

  Anna Latitia Waring, 1850–1860.

Z

D. 8. 6. 8. 6.

FATHER of Love, our Guide and Friend,
　O lead us gently on,
Until life's trial-time shall end,
　And heavenly peace be won !
We know not what the path may be
　As yet by us untrod ;
But we can trust our all to Thee,
　Our Father and our God !

If called, like Abraham's child, to climb
　The hill of sacrifice,
Some angel may be there in time ;
　Deliverance shall arise :
Or, if some darker lot be good,
　O teach us to endure
The sorrow, pain, or solitude,
　That make the spirit pure !

Christ by no flowery pathway came ;
　And we, His followers here,
Must do Thy will and praise Thy name,
　In hope, and love, and fear.
And, till in heaven we sinless bow,
　And faultless anthems raise,
O Father, Son, and Spirit, now
　Accept our feeble praise !

W. J. Irons (1812-1883).

15

Six 7's.

FOR the beauty of the earth,
  For the glory of the skies,
For the love which from our birth
  Over and around us lies,
Lord of all, to Thee we raise
This our hymn of grateful praise !

For the wonder of each hour
  Of the day and of the night,
Hill and vale, and tree and flower,
  Sun and moon, and stars of light,
Lord of all, to Thee we raise
This our hymn of grateful praise !

For the joy of human love,
  Brother, sister, parent, child,
Friends on earth, and friends above,
  Pleasures pure and undefiled,
Lord of all, to Thee we raise
This our hymn of grateful praise !

For each perfect gift of Thine
  To our race so freely given,
Graces human and divine,
  Flowers of earth, and buds of heaven.
Lord of all, to Thee we raise
This our hymn of grateful praise !

For Thy Church that evermore
  Lifteth holy hands above,
Offering up on every shore
  Her pure sacrifice of love,
Lord of all, to Thee we raise
This our hymn of grateful praise !

F. S. Pierpoint.

Z 2

16

7. 7. 7. 5.

GRACIOUS SPIRIT, Holy Ghost,
Taught by Thee, we covet most,
Of Thy gifts at Pentecost,
   Holy, heavenly love.

Love is kind, and suffers long,
Love is meek, and thinks no wrong,
Love than death itself more strong ;
 . Therefore give us love.

Prophecy will fade away,
Melting in the light of day ;
Love will ever with us stay ;
   Therefore give us love.

Faith will vanish into sight,
Hope be emptied in delight,
Love in heaven will shine more bright ;
   Therefore give us love.

Faith and hope and love we see
Joining hand in hand agree ;
But the greatest of the three,
   And the best, is love.

From the overshadowing
Of Thy gold and silver wing
Shed on us, who to Thee sing,
   Holy, heavenly love.

   Bp. Chr. Wordsworth (1807-1885), 1862.

17

Four 7's.

HARK, my soul! it is the Lord ;
'Tis thy Saviour—hear His word,
Jesus speaks, and speaks to thee :
" Say, poor sinner, lov'st thou Me ?

" I delivered thee when bound,
And, when bleeding, healed thy wound,
Sought thee wandering, set thee right,
Turned thy darkness into light.

" Can a woman's tender care
Cease toward the child she bare ?
Yes, she may forgetful be,
Yet will I remember thee.

" Mine is an unchanging love,
Higher than the heights above,
Deeper than the depths beneath,
Free and faithful, strong as death.

" Thou shalt see My glory soon,
When the work of grace is done ;
Partner of My throne shalt be :
Say, poor sinner, lov'st thou Me ? "

Lord, it is my chief complaint,
That my love is weak and faint :
Yet I love Thee and adore—
Oh ! for grace to love Thee more !

William Cowper (1731-1800), 1771.

18

HOW dare we pray Thee dwell within
These hearts defiled by wilful sin?
Yet, Holy Ghost, do not depart,
Leave not to earth our earthly heart;
And if Thou seest us erring still,
O bend to Thine our stubborn will,
And bring us to the fold again,
If need, by chastisement and pain.

Bring us, by all the powers of sense,
By all the course of Providence,
By inmost conscience, not yet dumb,
By all the past, by all to come,
By God's best gifts, His Son to die,
And Thee, our hearts to sanctify;
Bring us, before our sun go down,
To bear the cross, to win the crown.

J. Keble (1792-1866).

19

Four 7's.

HOLY SPIRIT, Truth divine !
Dawn upon this soul of mine ;
Voice of God, and inward Light,
Wake my spirit, clear my sight.

Holy Spirit, Love divine !
Glow within this heart of mine :
Kindle every high desire,
Perish self in Thy pure fire.

Holy Spirit, Power divine !
Fill and nerve this will of mine :
By Thee may I strongly live,
Bravely bear and nobly strive.

Holy Spirit, Right divine !
Reign within this soul of mine :
Be my law, and I shall be
Firmly bound, for ever free.

Holy Spirit, Peace divine !
Still this restless heart of mine :
Speak to calm this tossing sea,
Stayed in Thy tranquillity.

Holy Spirit, Joy divine !
Gladden Thou this heart of mine ;
In the desert ways I sing
" Spring, O well ! for ever spring."

Samuel Longfellow.

D. C. M.

I HEARD the voice of Jesus say
  " Come unto Me and rest ;
Lay down, thou weary one, lay down,
  Thy head upon My breast."
I came to Jesus as I was,
  Weary and worn and sad,
I found in Him a resting-place,
  And He has made me glad.

I heard the voice of Jesus say
  " Behold, I freely give
The living water ; thirsty one,
  Stoop down and drink and live."
I came to Jesus, and I drank
  Of that life-giving stream,
My thirst was quenched, my soul revived.
  And now I live in Him.

I heard the voice of Jesus say
  " I am this dark world's Light,
Look unto Me, thy morn shall rise,
  And all thy day be bright."
I looked to Jesus and I found
  In Him my Star, my Sun ;
And in that light of life I'll walk,
  Till travelling days are done.

Horatius Bonar, 1850.

21

C. M.

JESUS, the very thought of Thee,
    With sweetness fills my breast ;
But sweeter far Thy face to see,
    And in Thy presence rest.

Nor voice can sing, nor heart can frame,
    Nor can the memory find
A sweeter sound than Thy blest Name,
    O Saviour of mankind !

O hope of every contrite heart,
    O joy of all the meek ;
To those who fall, how kind Thou art !
    How good to those who seek !

But what to those who find ! Ah ! this
    Nor tongue nor pen can show !
The love of Jesus—what it is
    None but His loved ones know.

Jesus, our only joy be Thou,
    As Thou our crown wilt be ;
Jesus, be Thou our glory now,
    And through eternity.

Trans. by E. Caswall (1849),
*from the ' Iubilus rhythmicus de nomine Iesu,'
by St. Bernard of Clairvaux* (1091-1153).

22

D. 6. 6. 10.

LO ! summer comes again ;
And after spring-tide rain
The quickening sunbeams flood the world with light :
See, high in night's clear skies,
The joy of longing eyes,
The moon of harvest shines serenely bright.

O Lord of heaven and earth,
Who givest joy and mirth,
Open our lips to shew Thy wondrous praise :
Our hearts are dull and cold,
We leave Thy love untold ;
O give us strength our anthems glad to raise.

Each month we sow or reap,
Each hour we toil or sleep,
Thou givest life and joy, and Thou alone :
O grant to each and all,
When death s dark shadows fall,
To stand true workers round our Master's throne.

So, life's long task-work o'er,
Set free for evermore
We shall sit down at Thy great harvest feast ;
Reaper and sower met,
The burning heat forget,
And taste God's love, the greatest as the least.

E. H. Plumptre.

23

11. 11. 11. 5.

LORD of our life and God of our salvation,
Star of our night and Hope of every nation,
Hear and receive Thy Church's supplication,
    Lord God Almighty.

Lord, Thou canst help when earthly armour faileth,
Lord, Thou canst save when deadly sin assaileth,
Lord, o'er Thy Rock nor death nor hell prevaileth ;
    Grant us Thy peace, Lord.

Grant us Thy help till foes are backward driven,
Grant them Thy truth, that they may be forgiven,
Grant peace on earth, and, after we have striven,
    Peace in Thy heaven !

P. Pusey (1799-1855),
based on M. A. von Loewenstern (1594-1648).

L. M.

O COME and mourn with me awhile,
O come ye to the Saviour's side ;
O come, together let us mourn :
Jesus, our Love, is crucified.

Have we no tears to shed for Him,
While soldiers scoff and Jews deride :
Ah ! look how patiently He hangs :
Jesus, our Love, is crucified.

Seven times He spake, seven words of love :
And all three hours His silence cried
For mercy on the souls of men :
Jesus, our Love, is crucified.

A broken heart, a fount of tears
Ask, and they will not be denied:
A broken heart love's cradle is :
Jesus, our Love, is crucified.

O love of God, O sin of man,
In this dread act your strength is tried :
And victory remains with Love ;
For He, our Love, is crucified.

F. W. Faber (1814-1863), 1849.

25

Three 8's.

O GOD of life, whose power benign
Doth o'er the world in mercy shine,
Accept our praise, for we are Thine.

O Father, Uncreated Lord,
Be Thou in every land adored,
Be Thou by all with faith implored.

O Son of God, for sinners slain,
We bless Thee, Lord, whose dying pain
For us did endless life regain.

O Holy Ghost, whose guardian care
Doth us for heavenly joys prepare,
May we in Thy communion share.

O Holy, Blessèd Trinity,
With faith we sinners bow to Thee ;
In us, O God, exalted be.

A. T. Russell.

26

7. 6. 7. 6.

O HAPPY band of pilgrims.
If onward ye will tread.
With Jesus as your Fellow
To Jesus as your Head !

O happy if ye labour
As Jesus did for men ;
O happy if ye hunger
As Jesus hungered then !

The Cross that Jesus carried,
He carried as your due :
The Crown that Jesus weareth
He weareth it for you.

The faith by which ye see Him,
The hope, in which ye yearn,
The love that through all troubles
To Him alone will turn,

The trials that beset you,
The sorrows ye endure,
The manifold temptations
That death alone can cure,

What are they but His jewels
Of right celestial worth ?
What are they but the ladder
Set up to heaven on earth ?

O happy band of pilgrims,
Look upward to the skies,
Where such a light affliction
Shall win so great a prize.

J. M. Neale (1818-1866),
based on St. Joseph of the Studium (ninth century

27

D. 7. 6. 7. 6.

O JESUS! I have promised
　To serve Thee to the end ;
Be Thou for ever near me,
　My Master and my Friend ;
I shall not fear the battle,
　If Thou art by my side,.
Nor wander from the pathway,
　If Thou wilt be my Guide.

O let me hear Thee speaking
　In accents clear and. still,
Above the storms of passion,
　The murmurs of self-will :
O speak ! to reassure me,
　To hasten or control ;
O speak ! to make me listen,
　Thou Guardian of my soul.

O Jesus! Thou hast promised,
　To all who follow Thee,
That where Thou art in glory
　There shall Thy servant be :
And, Jesus, I have promised,
　To serve Thee to the end :
O give me grace to follow,
　My Master and my Friend !

O let me see Thy footmarks,
　And in them plant my own ;
My hope to follow duly
　Is in Thy strength alone :
O guide me, call me, draw me,
　Uphold me to the end ;
And then in heaven receive me,
　My Saviour and my Friend !

　　J. E. Bode (1816-1874), 1860.

28

T. 6. 5. 6. 5

ONWARD, Christian soldiers,
　Marching as to war,
With the Cross of Jesus
　Going on before :
Christ, the Royal Master
　Leads against the foe;
Forward into battle
　See His banners go.

　　Onward, Christian soldiers,
　　　Marching as to war,
　　With the Cross of Jesus
　　　Going on before.

At the sign of triumph
　Satan's host doth flee,
On then, Christian soldiers,
　On to victory !
Hell's foundations quiver
　At the shout of praise ;
Brothers, lift your voices,
　Loud your anthems raise.
　　　　Onward, &c.

Like a mighty army
　Moves the Church of God ;
Brothers, we are treading
　Where the saints have trod ;
We are not divided,
　All one body we,
One in hope, and doctrine,
　One in charity.
　　　　Onward, &c.

Crowns and thrones may perish,
  Kingdoms rise and wane,
But the Church of Jesus
  Constant will remain ;
Gates of hell can never
  'Gainst that Church prevail ;
We have Christ's own promise,
  And that cannot fail.
      Onward, &c.

Onward then, ye people,
  Join our happy throng ;
Blend with ours your voices
  In the triumph-song ;
Glory, laud, and honour,
  Unto Christ the King,
This through countless ages
  Men and Angels sing.
      Onward, &c.

      S. Baring-Gould, 1865.

29

L. M.

SING to the Lord a joyful song,
Lift up your hearts, your voices raise ;
To us His gracious gifts belong,
To Him our songs of love and praise.

For life and love, for rest and food,
For daily help, and nightly care,
Sing to the Lord, for He is good,
And praise His Name, for it is fair.

For strength to those who on Him wait,
His truth to prove, His will to do,
Praise ye our God, for He is great ;
Trust in His Name, for it is true.

For joys untold that daily move
Round those who love His sweet employ,
Sing to our God, for He is love ;
Exalt His Name, for it is joy.

Sing to the Lord of heaven and earth,
Whom angels serve and saints adore,
The Father, Son, and Holy Ghost,
To whom be praise for evermore.

J. S. B. Monsell (1811-1875), 1862.

30

D. 4. 6. 4. 6.

SLEEP thy last sleep,
Free from care and sorrow ;
  Rest, where none weep,
Till the eternal morrow ;
  Though dark waves roll
O'er the silent river,
  Thy fainting soul
Jesus can deliver.

  Life's dream is past,
All its sin, its sadness ;
  Brightly at last
Dawns a day of gladness.
  Under thy sod,
Earth, receive our treasure,
  To rest in God,
Waiting all His pleasure.

  Though we may mourn
Those in life the dearest,
  They shall return,
Christ, when Thou appearest !
  Soon shall Thy voice
Comfort those now weeping,
  Bidding rejoice
All in Jesus sleeping.

E. A. Dayman.

31

Four 7's.

SOLDIERS, who are Christ's below,
Strong in faith resist the foe :
Boundless is the pledged reward
Unto them who serve the Lord.

'Tis no palm of fading leaves
That the conqueror's hand receives ;
Joys are his serene and pure,
Light that ever shall endure.

For the souls that overcome
Waits the beauteous heavenly home,
Where the blessèd evermore
Tread on high the starry floor.

Passing soon and little worth
Are the things that tempt on earth ;
Heavenward lift thy soul's regard ;
God Himself is thy reward.

Father, who the crown dost give,
Saviour, by whose death we live,
Spirit, who our hearts dost raise,
Three in One, Thy name we praise.

J. H. Clark, 1868,
from the Latin (Paris Breviary).

32

6. 5. 6. 5.

SUMMER suns are glowing
  Over land and sea,
Happy light is flowing
  Bountiful and free.

God's free mercy streameth
  Over all the world,
And His banner gleameth
  Everywhere unfurled.

Lord, upon our blindness
  Thy pure radiance pour ;
For Thy loving-kindness
  Makes us love Thee more.

And when clouds are drifting
  Dark across our sky,
Then, the veil uplifting,
  Father, be Thou nigh.

We will never doubt Thee,
  Though Thou veil Thy light ;
Life is dark without Thee ;
  Death with Thee is bright.

Light of Light ! shine o'er us,
  On our pilgrim way ;
Go Thou still before us,
  To the endless day.

Bishop Walsham How.

33

D. 7. 6. 8. 6.

TEN thousand times ten thousand,
    In sparkling raiment bright,
The armies of the ransomed saints
    Throng up the steeps of light :
'Tis finished ! all is finished,
    Their fight with death and sin ;
Fling open wide the golden gates,
    And let the victors in !

What rush of hallelujahs
    Fills all the earth and sky !
What ringing of a thousand harps
    Bespeaks the triumph nigh !
O day for which creation
    And all its tribes were made !
O joy, for all its former woes
    A thousandfold repaid !

Oh, then, what raptured greetings
    On Canaan's happy shore !
What knitting severed friendships up,
    Where partings are no more !
Then eyes with joy shall sparkle
    That brimmed with tears of late,
Orphans no longer fatherless,
    Nor widows desolate.

Bring near Thy great salvation,
    Thou Lamb for sinners slain ;
Fill up the roll of Thine elect,
    Then take Thy power and reign ;
Appear, Desire of nations,
    Thine exiles long for home ;
Show in the heavens Thy promised sign,
    Thou Prince and Saviour, come.

Dean Alford (1810-1871), 1867.

34

7. 6. 7. 6.

THE year is swiftly waning;
　The summer days are past ;
And life, brief life, is speeding ;
　The end is nearing fast.

The ever-changing seasons
　In silence come and go ;
But Thou, Eternal Father,
　No time or change canst know.

O pour Thy grace upon us,
　That we may worthier be,
Each year that passes o'er us,
　To dwell in heaven with Thee.

O by each mercy sent us,
　And by each grief and pain ;
By blessings like the sunshine,
　And sorrows like the rain,

Our barren hearts make fruitful
　With every goodly grace,
That we Thy Name may hallow,
　And see at last Thy face.

Bishop Walsham How.

35

L. M.

THIS day, by Thy creative Word
First o'er the earth the light was poured ;
O Lord, this day upon us shine,
And fill our souls with light divine.

This day the Lord, for sinners slain,
In might victorious rose again ;
O Jesu, may we raisèd be
From death of sin to life in Thee.

This day the Holy Spirit came
With fiery tongues of cloven flame ;
O Spirit, fill our hearts this day
With grace to hear, and grace to pray.

O day of light and life and grace,
From earthly toils sweet resting place !
Thy hallowed hours, best gift of love,
We give again to God above !

Bishop Walsham How.

36

8. 7. 8. 7.

THROUGH the night of doubt and sorrow
  Onward goes the pilgrim band,
Singing songs of expectation,
  Marching to the Promised Land.

Clear before us through the darkness
  Gleams and burns the guiding light ;
Brother clasps the hand of brother,
  Stepping fearless through the night.

One the Light of God's own Presence,
  O'er His ransomed people shed,
Chasing far the gloom and terror,
  Brightening all the path we tread ;

One the object of our journey,
  One the faith which never tires,
One the earnest looking forward,
  One the hope our God inspires ;

One the gladness of rejoicing
  On the far, eternal shore,
Where the one Almighty Father
  Reigns in love for evermore.

Trans. by S. Baring-Gould,
from German of B. S. Ingemann (1789-1862) ·

37

Four 6's.

THY Kingdom come, O God,
  Thy rule, O Christ, begin ;
Break with Thine iron rod
  The tyrannies of sin.

Where is Thy reign of peace,
  And purity, and love ?
When shall all hatred cease,
  As in the realms above ?

When comes the promised time
  That war shall be no more,
Oppression, lust, and crime
  Shall flee Thy face before ?

We pray Thee, Lord, arise,
  And come in Thy great might ;
Revive our longing eyes,
  Which languish for Thy sight.

O'er heathen lands afar
  Thick darkness broodeth yet :
Arise, O Morning Star,
  Arise, and never set.

Lewis Hensley.

38

L. M.

WHERE high the heavenly temple stands,
The house of God, not made with hands,
A great High Priest our nature wears,
The Guardian of mankind appears.

He, who for men their surety stood,
And poured on earth His precious Blood,
Pursues in heaven His mighty plan,
The Saviour and the Friend of man.

In every pang that rends the heart,
The Man of Sorrows had a part ;
Touched with the feeling of our grief,
He to the sufferer sends relief.

With boldness, therefore, at the Throne
Let us make all our sorrows known,
And ask the aid of heavenly power
To help us in the evil hour.

M. Bruce (1746-1767).

39

S. M.

YE servants of the Lord,
  Each in his office wait,
Observant of His heavenly word,
  And watchful at His gate.

Let all your lamps be bright,
  And trim the golden flame ;
Gird up your loins, as in His sight,
  For awful is His Name.

Watch : 'tis your Lord's command,
  And, while we speak, He's near :
Mark the first signal of His hand,
  And ready all appear.

O happy servant he
  In such a posture found !
He shall his Lord with rapture see,
  And be with honour crowned.

Christ shall the banquet spread
  With His own royal hand ;
And raise that faithful servant's head
  Amid the angelic band.

To God, the Father, Son,
  And Spirit, ever blest,
The One in Three, the Three in One,
  Be endless praise addressed.

Varied from P. Doddridge (1702-1751).

APPENDIX II.

SACRED POEMS.

I

BROTHER, hast thou wandered far
  From thy Father's happy home,
With thyself and God at war?
  Turn thee, brother, homeward come

Hast thou wasted all the powers
  God for nobler uses gave?
Squandered life's most golden hours?
  Turn thee, brother, God can save!

Is a mighty famine now
  In thy heart and in thy soul?
Discontent upon thy brow?
  Turn thee: God will make thee whole.

F. F. Clarke, 1856.

2

D. 8. 7.

BROTHER, thou art gone before us,
  And thy saintly soul is flown
Where tears are wiped from every eye,
  And sorrow is unknown ;
From the burthen of the flesh,
  And from care and fear released,
Where the wicked cease from troubling,
  And the weary are at rest.

The toilsome way thou'st travell'd o'er,
  And borne the heavy load ;
But Christ hath taught thy languid feet
  To reach His blest abode.
Thou'rt sleeping now, like Lazarus
  Upon his father's breast,
Where the wicked cease from troubling,
  And the weary are at rest.

Sin can never taint thee now,
  Nor doubt thy faith assail,
Nor thy meek trust in Jesus Christ
  And the Holy Spirit fail :
And there thou'rt sure to meet the good,
  Whom on earth thou lovedst best,
Where the wicked cease from troubling,
  And the weary are at rest.

" Earth to earth," and " Dust to dust,"
　　The solemn words are said ;
So we lay the turf above thee now,
　　And we seal thy narrow bed :
But thy spirit, brother, soars away
　　Among the faithful blest,
Where the wicked cease from troubling,
　　And the weary are at rest.

And when the Lord shall summon us,
　　Whom thou hast left behind,
May we, untainted by the world,
　　As sure a welcome find
May each, like thee, depart in peace,
　　To be a glorious guest,
Where the wicked cease from troubling,
　　And the weary are at rest.

　　　　　　　　Dean Milman (1791-1868).

3

ECCE panis Angelorum,
Factus cibus viatorum,
Vere panis filiorum,
    Non mittendus canibus.
In figuris praesignatur,
Cum Isaac immolatur,
Agnus Paschae deputatur,
    Datur manna patribus.

Bone pastor, panis vere,
Iesu, nostri miserere,
Tu nos pasce, nos tuere,
Tu nos bona fac videre
    In terra viventium.
Tu, qui cuncta scis et vales,
Qui nos pascis hic mortales,
Tu nos ibi commensales,
Coheredes et sodales
    Fac sanctorum civium.

From the Lauda Sion of St. Thomas Aquinas
                    (1227-1274), 1261.

4

ECCE Quem vates vetustis
  Concinebant saeculis,
Quem Prophetarum fideles
  Paginae spoponderant ;
Emicat promissus olim,
  Cuncta collaudant eum
    Saeculorum saeculis.

Psallat altitudo coeli,
  Psallant omnes angeli,
Quicquid est virtutis usquam
  Psallat in laudem Dei,
Nulla linguarum silescat
  Vox et omnis consonet
    Saeculorum saeculis.

5

COME, O Thou Traveller unknown !
  Whom still I hold, but cannot see,
My company before is gone,
  And I am left alone with Thee :
With Thee all night I mean to stay,
And wrestle till the break of day.

Wilt thou not yet to me reveal
  Thy new, unutterable Name?
Tell me, I still beseech Thee, tell !
  To know it now, resolved I am :
Wrestling, I will not let Thee go,
Till I Thy Name, Thy Nature know.

Yield to me now, for I am weak,
  But confident in self-despair ;
Speak to my heart, in blessings speak,
  Be conquered by my instant prayer !
Speak, or Thou never hence shalt move,
And tell me if Thy Name is Love !

My prayer hath power with God ; the grace
  Unspeakable I now receive ;
Through faith I see Thee face to face,
  I see Thee face to face, and live :
In vain I have not wept and strove ;
Thy Nature, and Thy Name, is Love.

I know Thee, Saviour ! who Thou art ;
  Jesus, the feeble sinner's Friend ;
Nor wilt Thou with the night depart,
  But stay, and love me to the end :
Thy mercies never shall remove ;
Thy Nature, and Thy Name, is Love !

                    C. *Wesley* (1708-1788).

6

DIES irae, dies illa
Solvet saeclum in favilla,
Teste David cum Sibylla.

Quantus tremor est futurus,
Quando iudex est venturus,
Cuncta stricte discussurus !

Tuba mirum spargens sonum
Per sepulcra regionum
Coget omnes ante thronum.

Mors stupebit et natura,
Cum resurget creatura
Iudicanti responsura.

Liber scriptus proferetur,
In quo totum continetur
Unde mundus iudicetur.

Iudex ergo cum sedebit,
Quidquid latet apparebit,
Nil inultum remanebit !

Quid sum miser tum dicturus ?
Quem patronum rogaturus,
Cum nec iustus sit securus ?

Rex tremendæ maiestatis !
Qui salvandos salvas gratis,
Salva me, fons pietatis !

Recordare, Iesu pie !
Quod sum causa tuae viae :
Ne me perdas illa die !

Quaerens me sedisti lassus ;
Redemisti, crucem passus ;
Tantus labor non sit cassus.

Iustae iudex ultionis,
Donum fac remissionis
Ante diem rationis.

Ingemisco tanquam reus,
Culpa rubet vultus meus :
Supplicanti parce, Deus !

Qui Mariam absolvisti,
Qui latronem exaudisti,
Mihi quoque spem dedisti.

Preces meae non sunt dignae,
Sed tu, Bone, fac benigne,
Ne perenni cremer igne.

Inter oves locum praesta,
Et ab haedis me sequestra,
Statuas in parte dextra.

Confutatis maledictis,
Flammis acribus addictis,
Voca me cum benedictis.

Oro supplex et acclinis,
Cor contritum, quasi cinis,
Gere curam mei finis.

   Thomas de Celano (thirteenth century).

GO, work for God, and do not say
  Thou canst not useful be :
A talent lies in every man,
  And one was hid in thee.

Be it in head, or heart, or hand,
  Search well, and thou shalt find
The lowliest life, by simple deeds,
  Can help and bless mankind.

It may be He hath sent thee forth,
  With wondrous wisdom stored,
To teach the longing soul to love
  The beauty of the Lord.

Or in thy hand the power may lie
  Eternal truths to write,
Whereby the darkness of the world
  May yield to heaven's light.

Or in His love He may have tuned
  The accents of thy voice,
To sing sweet songs of sympathy,
  And make sad hearts rejoice.

Then speak, or write, or sing for God :
  Do something, do it well ;
And by an earnest, holy life
  Thy Maker's goodness tell.

Thus toil for Him, and thou shalt reach
  Thy God-appointed place ;
And when thy working days are o'er
  Thou shalt behold His face.

Edwin Hodder, 1871.

8

GOD draws a cloud over each gleaming morn ;
    Would we ask why ?
It is because all noblest things are born
    In agony.

Only upon some cross of pain or woe
    God's sons may lie ;
Each soul redeemed from sin and self must know
    Its Calvary.

God never sends a joy not meant in love,
    Still less a pain ;
Our gratitude the sunlight falls to prove,
    Our faith the rain.

And neither life, nor death, nor things below,
    Nor things above,
Shall ever sever us that we should go
    From His great love.

Frances Power Cobbe.

9

GOD of the living, in whose eyes
Unveiled Thy whole creation lies ;
All souls are Thine ; we must not say
That those are dead who pass away ;
From this our world of flesh set free,
We know them living unto Thee.

Released from earthly toil and strife,
With Thee is hidden still their life ;
Thine are their thoughts, their works, their powers,
All Thine, and yet most truly ours ;
For well we know, where'er they be,
Our dead are living unto Thee.

Not spilt like water on the ground,
Not wrapped in dreamless sleep profound,
Not wand'ring in unknown despair
Beyond Thy voice, Thine arm, Thy care ;
Not left to die like fallen tree ;
Not dead, but living unto Thee.

O Breather into man of breath,
O Holder of the keys of death,
O Giver of the life within,
Save us from death, the death of sin ;
That body, soul, and spirit be
For ever living unto Thee.

J. Ellerton.

HARK ! the sound of holy voices
 Chanting, at the crystal sea,
Alleluia, Alleluia,
 Alleluia, Lord, to Thee :
Multitude, which none can number,
 Like the stars in glory stands,
Clothed in white apparel, holding
 Palms of victory in their hands.

Patriarch and holy Prophet,
 Who prepared the way of Christ,
King, Apostle, Saint, Confessor,
 Martyr, and Evangelist,
Saintly Maiden, godly Matron,
 Widows who have watched to prayer,
Joined in holy concert, singing
 To the Lord of all, are there.

They have come from tribulation,
 And have washed their robes in blood,
Washed them in the blood of Jesus ;
 Tried they were, and firm they stood ;
Mocked, imprisoned, stoned, tormented,
 Sawn asunder, slain with sword,
They have conquered death and Satan
 By the might of Christ the Lord.

Marching with Thy Cross their banner,
 They have triumphed, following
Thee, the Captain of Salvation,
 Thee, their Saviour, and their King :
Gladly, Lord, with Thee they suffered,
 Gladly, Lord, with Thee they died ;
And by death to life immortal
 They were born and glorified.

Now they reign in heavenly glory,
  Now they walk in golden light,
Now they drink, as from a river,
  Holy bliss and infinite :
Love and peace they taste for ever,
  And all truth and knowledge see
In the Beatific Vision
  Of the blessèd Trinity.

God of God, the One-begotten,
  Light of Light, Immanuel,
In whose Body joined together
  All the saints for ever dwell ;
Pour upon us of Thy fulness,
  That we may for evermore
Thee with Thine Eternal Father
  And the Holy Ghost adore.

Bishop Chr. Wordsworth (1807 1885).

HE leads us on
By paths we did not know ;
Upward He leads us though our steps be slow,
Though oft we faint and falter on the way,
Though storms and darkness oft obscure the day,
   Yet when the clouds are gone,
   We know He leads us on.

He leads us on
Through all th' unquiet years ;
Past all our dreamland hopes, and doubts, and
      fears,
He guides our steps, through all the tangled maze
Of losses, sorrows, and o'erclouded days ;
   We know His will is done,
   And still He leads us on.

And He, at last,
After the weary strife,
After the restless fever we call life,
After the dreariness, the aching pain,
The wayward struggles, which have proved in vain,
   After our toils are past
   Will give us rest at last.

*Trans. by J. Borthwick, from
the German of Count von Zinzendorf* (1700-1765).

12

HERE, O my Lord, I see Thee face to face ;
  Here faith can touch and handle things unseen ;
Here would I grasp with firmer hand Thy grace,
  And all my weariness upon Thee lean.

Here would I feed upon the bread of God ;
  Here drink with Thee the royal wine of heaven ;
Here would I lay aside each earthly load ;
  Here taste afresh the calm of sin forgiven.

I have no help but Thine, nor do I need
  Another arm save Thine to lean upon ;
It is enough, my Lord, enough indeed ;
  My strength is in Thy might, Thy might alone.

Mine is the sin, but Thine the righteousness ;
  Mine is the guilt, but Thine the cleansing blood :
Here is my robe, my refuge, and my peace—
  Thy blood, Thy righteousness, O Lord, my God.

Too soon we rise ; the symbols disappear ;
  The feast, though not the love, is past and gone ;
The bread and wine remove, but Thou art here
  Nearer than ever—still my Shield and Sun.

Feast after feast thus comes and passes by,
  Yet passing points to the glad feast above,
Giving sweet fore-tastes of the festal joy,
  The Lamb's great bridal-feast of bliss and love.

Horatius Bonar.

HORA novissima, tempora pessima sunt, vigilemus!
Ecce minaciter imminet Arbiter Ille supremus:
Imminet, imminet, ut mala terminet, aequa coronet,
Recta remuneret, anxia liberet, aethera donet.
Auferat aspera duraque pondera mentis onustae,
Sobria muniat, improba puniat, utraque iuste.
Ille piissimus, ille gravissimus, ecce venit Rex:
Surgat homo reus, instat Homo Deus, a Patre
    Iudex.

      *   *   *   *   *

Urbs Syon inclyta, turris et edita littore tuto,
Te peto, te colo, te flagro, te volo, canto, saluto:
Nec meritis peto; nam meritis meto morte perire:
Nec reticens tego, quod meritis ego filius irae.
Vita quidem mea, vita nimis rea, mortua vita,
Quippe reatibus exitialibus obruta, trita.
Spe tamen ambulo, praemia postulo speque fideque;
Illa perennia postulo praemia nocte dieque:
Me Pater optimus atque piissimus ille creavit,
In lue pertulit, ex lue sustulit, a lue lavit.
Dum sua suppleo robora, gaudeo: cum mea ploro,
Tunc sibi gaudeo, tunc mihi defleo, flere laboro:
Diluit omnia coelica gratia, Fons David undans,
Omnia diluit, omnibus affluit, omnia mundans.

O mea, spes mea, tu Syon aurea, clarior auro,
Agmine splendida, stans duce florida perpete lauro;
O bona Patria, num tua gaudia teque videbo?
O bona Patria, num tua praemia plena tenebo?

*From the rhythm of Bernard of Cluny on the
Heavenly Country (twelfth century).*

14

I BRING my sins to Thee,
 The sins I cannot count,
That all may cleansèd be
 In Thy once opened Fount :
I bring them. Saviour, all to Thee,
The burden is too great for me.

My heart to Thee I bring,
 The heart I cannot read ;
A faithless wandering thing,
 An evil heart indeed :
I bring it. Saviour, now to Thee,
That fixed and faithful it may be.

To Thee I bring my care,
 The care I cannot flee ;
Thou wilt not only share,
 But bear it all for me :
O loving Saviour, now to Thee
I bring the load that wearies me.

I bring my grief to Thee,
 The grief I cannot tell ;
No words shall needed be,
 Thou knowest all so well :
I bring the sorrow laid on me,
O suffering Saviour, now to Thee.

My joys to Thee I bring,
   The joys Thy love hath given,
That each may be a wing
   To lift me nearer heaven :
I bring them, Saviour, all to Thee,
For Thou hast purchased all for me.

My life I bring to Thee,
   I would not be my own ;
O Saviour, let me be
   Thine ever, Thine alone :
My heart, my life, my all I bring
To Thee, my Saviour and my King !

Frances Ridley Havergal (1836-1879), 1870

15

I GAVE My life for thee,
   My precious blood I shed,
That thou might'st ransomed be,
   And quickened from the dead :
I gave My life for thee ;
What hast thou given for Me ?

I spent long years for thee,
   In weariness and woe,
That an eternity
   Of joy thou mightest know :
I spent long years for thee ;
Hast thou spent one for Me ?

My Father's home of light,
   My rainbow-circled throne,
I left for earthly night,
   For wanderings sad and lone :
I left it all for thee ;
Hast thou left aught for Me ?

I suffered much for thee,
   More than thy tongue may tell,
Of bitterest agony,
   To rescue thee from hell :
I suffered much for thee ;
What canst thou bear for Me ?

And I have brought to thee,
   Down from My home above,
Salvation full and free,
   My pardon and My love :
Great gifts I brought to thee ;
What hast thou brought to Me ?

Oh ! let thy life be given,
   Thy years for Him be spent,
World-fetters all be riven,
   And joy with suffering blent :
I gave Myself for thee ;
Give thou thyself to Me !

Frances Ridley Havergal (1836-1879), 1859.

I GIVE my heart to Thee,
  O Jesus most desired !
And heart for heart the gift shall be,
  For Thou my soul hast fired ;
  Thou hearts alone wouldst move,
  Thou only hearts dost love ;
I would love Thee as Thou lov'st me,
  O Jesus most desired !

What offering can I make,
  Dear Lord, to love like Thine ?
That Thou, the Word, didst stoop to take
  A human form like mine !
  " Give Me thy heart, My son : "
  Lord, Thou my heart hast won ;
I would love Thee as Thou lov'st me,
  O Jesus most desired !

Here finds my heart its rest,
  Repose that knows no shock,
The strength of love that keeps it blest
  In Thee, the riven Rock :
  My soul, as girt around,
  Her citadel hath found :
I would love Thee as Thou lov'st me,
  O Jesus most desired !

Ancient Latin Hymn,
trans. by Ray Palmer, 1868.

17

IESU dulcis memoria,
Dans vera cordis gaudia,
Sed super mel et omnia
Dulcis eius praesentia.

Nil canitur suavius,
Auditur nil iucundius,
Nil cogitatur dulcius
Quam Iesus Dei Filius.

Iesu, spes poenitentibus,
Quam pius es petentibus,
Quam bonus es quaerentibus
Sed quid invenientibus?

Nec lingua potest dicere,
Nec littera exprimere,
Experto potes credere,
Quid sit Iesum diligere.

Sis, Iesu, nostrum gaudium,
Qui es futurus praemium ;
Sit nostra in te gloria
Per cuncta semper saecula.

From the ' Iubilus rhythmicus de nomine Iesu,'
or ' De aeterna sapientia,' of St. Bernard of
Clairvaux (1091-1153), 1140.

18

JESUS, and shall it ever be!
A mortal man ashamed of Thee!
Ashamed of Thee, whom angels praise,
Whose glories shine to endless days.

Ashamed of Jesus! sooner far
Let evening blush to own a star:
He sheds His beams of light divine
O'er this benighted soul of mine.

Ashamed of Jesus! just as soon
Let midnight be ashamed of noon:
'Tis midnight with my soul till He,
Bright morning star, bids darkness flee.

Ashamed of Jesus! that dear Friend,
On whom my hopes of heaven depend!
No!—when I blush, be this my shame,
That I no more revere His name.

Ashamed of Jesus! yes, I may,
When I've no guilt to wash away,
No tear to wipe, no good to crave,
No fears to quell, no soul to save.

Till then,—nor is my boasting vain,—
Till then, I boast a Saviour slain:
And O! may this my glory be,
That Christ is not ashamed of me!

J. Grigg, 1765.

19

LET us with a gladsome mind
Praise the Lord, for He is kind !
Long our island throne has stood,
Planted on the ocean flood ;
Crowned with rock, and girt with sea,
Home and refuge of the free :
For His mercies aye endure,
Ever faithful, ever sure.

On that Island throne have sate
Alfred's goodness, Edward's state ;
Princely strength and queenly grace,
Lengthened line of royal race :
Round that throne have stood of old
Seers and statesmen, firm and bold ;
Burghley's wisdom, Hampden's fire,
Chatham's force in son and sire.

Let us with a gladsome mind
Praise the Lord, for He is kind !
Him, in homely English tongue,
Epic lay and lyric song,
Shakespeare's myriad-minded verse,
Milton's heavenward strains, rehearse :
For His mercies aye endure,
Ever faithful, ever sure.

Let us with a gladsome mind
Praise the Lord, for He is kind !
Soldiers tried in every clime,
Sailors famous through all time ;
Hands of iron, hearts of oak,
Fresh from their Creator's stroke ;
These His gifts for aye endure,
Ever faithful, ever sure.

Science, with her thousand eyes,
Sunless mine and starlit skies
Probes and pierces, far and near,
Man's estate to guide and cheer :
Hither, in our heathen night,
Came of yore the Gospel light ;
By the Saviour's sacred story
"Angles" turned to Angels' glory.

Let us with a gladsome mind
Praise the Lord, for He is kind !
Rustic churchyard, lordly pile,
Studious cloister, crowded aisle,
Lady chapel, gorgeous shrine,
All proclaim with voice divine
That Thy mercies still endure,
Ever faithful, ever sure.

Let us with a gladsome mind
Praise the Lord, for He is kind !
Breaking with a gracious hand
Ancient error's subtle band,
Opening wide the sacred page,
Kindling hope in saint and sage ;
For His mercies aye endure,
Ever faithful, ever sure.

Give us homes serene and pure,
Settled freedom, laws secure,
Truthful lips, and mind sincere,
Faith and love that cast out fear :
Grant that Light and Life Divine
Long on England's shores may shine ;
Grant that People, Church, and Throne
May in all good deeds be one !

Dean Stanley (1815-1881).

20

"LORD, and what shall this man do?"
  Askest thou, Christian, for thy friend?
If his love for Christ be true,
  Christ hath told thee of his end:
This is he whom God approves,
This is he whom Jesus loves.

Ask not of him more than this,
  Leave it in his Saviour's breast,
Whether, early call'd to bliss,
  He in youth shall find his rest,
Or armed in his station wait,
Till his Lord be at the gate.

Whether in his lonely course
  (Lonely, not forlorn) he stay,
Or with love's supporting force
  Cheat the toil, and cheer the way:
Leave it all in His high hand,
Who doth hearts as streams command.

Gales from heaven, if so He will,
  Sweeter melodies can wake
In the lonely mountain rill,
  Than the meeting waters make:
Who hath the Father and the Son
May be left, but not alone.

Sick or healthful, slave or free,
  Wealthy, or despised and poor—
What is that to him or thee,
  So his love to Christ endure?
When the shore is won at last,
Who will count the billows past?

Only, since our souls will shrink
  At the touch of natural grief,
When our earthly loved ones sink,
  Send us, Lord, Thy sure relief;
Patient hearts, their pain to see,
And Thy grace, to follow Thee.

  John Keble (1792-1866).

MY God, I love Thee, not because
   I hope for heaven thereby ;
Nor yet because who love Thee not
   Are lost eternally.

Then why, O blessèd Jesus Christ,
   Why do I love Thee well ?
Not for the sake of winning heaven,
   Nor of escaping hell ;

Not with the hope of gaining aught
   Nor seeking a reward ;
But as Thyself hast lovèd me,
   O ever loving Lord !

E'en so I love Thee and will love,
   And in Thy praise will sing,
Solely because Thou art my God,
   And my most loving King.

Trans. by E. Caswall,
from the Latin of Francis Xavier (1506-1552).

22

MY God, I thank Thee, who hast made
 The earth so bright :
So full of splendour and of joy,
 Beauty and light ;
So many glorious things are here,
 Noble and right !

I thank Thee, too, that Thou hast made
 Joy to abound ;
So many gentle thoughts and deeds
 Circling us round,
That in the darkest spot of earth
 Some love is found.

I thank Thee more that all our joy
 Is touched with pain ;
That shadows fall on brightest hours,
 That thorns remain ;
So that earth's bliss may be our guide
 And not our chain.

For Thou who knowest, Lord, how soon
 Our weak heart clings,
Hast given us joys, tender and true,
 Yet all with wings ;
So that we see, gleaming on high,
 Diviner things.

I thank Thee, Lord, that Thou hast kept
 The best in store ;
We have enough, yet not too much
 To long for more ;
A yearning for a deeper peace
 Not known before.

I thank Thee, Lord, that here our souls,
 Though amply blest,
Can never find, although they seek,
 A perfect rest ;
Nor ever shall, until they lean
 On Jesus' breast.

     A. A. Procter (1825-1864).

23

MY God (O let me call Thee mine !
  Weak, wretched sinner though I be),
My trembling soul would fain be Thine ;
  My feeble faith still clings to Thee.

Not only for the past I grieve,
  The future fills me with dismay ;
Unless Thou hasten to relieve,
  Thy suppliant is a castaway.

I cannot say my faith is strong,
  I dare not hope my love is great ;
But strength and hope to Thee belong :
  O do not leave me desolate !

I know I owe my all to Thee ;
  O take the heart I cannot give !
Do Thou my strength, my Saviour be,
  And make me to Thy glory live.

Anne Bronte (1820-1849,.

24

MY Lord, my God ! If fear or shame
  Drive from my lips Thy praise divine ;
If, when a cold world scorns Thy name,
  I stand not forth to own Thee mine ;
If faithless doubts my soul assail,
  Or sins have made me false to Thee ;
As once on Thy disciple frail,
  So turn, dear Lord, and look on me.

Cast but one kind reproachful look,
  And make me all the past recall,
Thy love that never me forsook,
  Thy grace that would not let me fall,
Thy life that taught me how to live,
  Thy death that conquered death for me :
O Lord, my wanderings past forgive !
  From such a friend no more I flee !

Oh, let me feel Thee watching still,
  With eyes that slumber not nor sleep ;
From every step in paths of ill
  That look shall call me back to weep.
Look ever on me, till I come
  Where I no more can fall from Thee ;
Then in the heavenly Father's home
  With Thy salvation look on me.

F. D. Maurice, ✠ 1872.

25

F OR a closer walk with God,
  A calm and heavenly frame !
A light to shine upon the road
  That leads me to the Lamb !

Where is the blessedness I knew
  When first I saw the Lord?
Where is the soul-refreshing view
  Of Jesus and His word?

What peaceful hours I once enjoy'd,
  How sweet their memory still !
But they have left an aching void
  The world can never fill.

Return, O Holy Dove, return,
  Sweet messenger of rest :
I hate the sins that made Thee mourn,
  And drove Thee from my breast.

The dearest idol I have known,
  Whate'er that idol be,
Help me to tear it from Thy throne,
  And worship only Thee.

So shall my walk be close with God,
  Calm and serene my frame ;
So purer light shall mark the road
  That leads me to the Lamb.

W. Cowper (1731-1800), 1772.

26

O GOD, who when the night was deep,
Hast kept me safe, and lent me sleep,
Now with Thy sun Thou bidd'st me rise,
And look around with older eyes.

Each blessèd morning Thou dost give,
I have one morning less to live ;
Oh, help me so this day to spend,
To make me fitter for the end.

Oh, bid all wicked thoughts to fly,
The fretful word, and idle eye ;
Help me to think, in all I do,
"God sees me :—would He have it so ?"

Make my first wish and thought to be
For others sooner than for me ;
And let me pardon them, as I
Hope for Thy pardon when I die.

Be with me when I work and play ;
Be with me now and every day ;
Be near me, when I pray Thee, hear ;
And when I pray not, Lord ! be near.

F. T. Palgrave.

27

O MASTER ! it is good to be
High on the mountain here with Thee ;
Where stand revealed to mortal gaze
Those glorious saints of other days,
Who once received on Horeb's height
The eternal laws of truth and right ;
Or caught the still small whisper, higher
Than storm, than earthquake, or than fire.

O Master ! it is good to be
With Thee, and with Thy faithful three,—
Here, where the apostle's heart of rock
Is nerved against temptation's shock ;
Here, where the son of thunder learns
The thought that breathes, the word that burns ;
Here, where on eagle's wings we move
With Him whose last best creed is love.

O Master ! it is good to be
Entranced, enwrapt, alone with Thee ;
And watch Thy glistering raiment glow,
Whiter than Hermon's whitest snow ;
The human lineaments that shine
Irradiant with a light divine :
Till we too change from grace to grace,
Gazing on that transfigured face.

O Master ! it is good to be
Here on the Holy Mount with Thee :
When darkling in the depths of night,
When dazzled with excess of light,
We bow before the heavenly voice
That bids bewildered souls rejoice,
Though love wax cold, and faith be dim—
"This is My Son—O hear ye Him."

Dean Stanley (1815-1881).

28

PRAYER is the soul's sincere desire,
  Utter'd or unexpress'd :
The motion of a hidden fire,
  That trembles in the breast.

Prayer is the burden of a sigh,
  The falling of a tear ;
The upward glancing of an eye,
  When none but God is near.

Prayer is the simplest form of speech
  That infant lips can try ;
Prayer the sublimest strains that reach
  The Majesty on high.

Prayer is the contrite sinner's voice,
  Returning from his ways ;
While angels in their songs rejoice,
  And cry, " Behold, he prays ! "

Prayer is the Christian's vital breath,
  The Christian's native air ;
His watchword at the gates of death ;
  He enters heaven with prayer.

The saints in prayer appear as one,
  In word, and deed, and mind,
While with the Father and the Son
  Sweet fellowship they find.

Nor prayer is made on earth alone ;
  The Holy Spirit pleads ;
And Jesus, on the eternal throne,
  For sinners intercedes.

O Thou, by Whom we come to God,
  The Life, the Truth, the Way !
The path of prayer Thyself hast trod :
  Lord, teach us how to pray !
      James Montgomery (1771-1854), 1818.

29

PRAISE to the Holiest in the height
  And in the depth be praise ;
In all His words most wonderful,
  Most sure in all His ways.

O loving wisdom of our God !
  When all was sin and shame,
A second Adam to the fight,
  And to the rescue came.

O wisest love ! that flesh and blood,
  Which did in Adam fail,
Should strive afresh against the foe,
  Should strive, and should prevail:

And that a higher gift than grace
  Should flesh and blood refine ;
God's Presence and His very Self,
  And Essence all-divine.

O generous love ! that He, who smote
  In man for man the foe,
The double agony in man
  For man should undergo ;

And in the garden secretly,
  And on the cross on high,
Should teach His brethren, and inspire
  To suffer and to die.

Praise to the Holiest in the height,
  And in the depth be praise ;
In all His words most wonderful,
  Most sure in all His ways.

J. H. Newman,
from " The Dream of Gerontius."

30

RESTING from His work to-day,
In the tomb the Saviour lay ;
Still He slept, from head to feet
Shrouded in the winding sheet,
Lying in the rock alone,
Hidden by the sealèd stone.

Late at even there was seen,
Watching long, the Magdalene ;
Early, ere the break of day,
Sorrowful, she took her way
To the holy garden glade,
Where her buried Lord was laid.

So with Thee, till life shall end,
I would solemn vigil spend ;
Let me hew Thee, Lord, a shrine
In this rocky heart of mine,
Where, in pure embalmèd cell,
None but Thou may ever dwell.

Myrrh and spices will I bring,
True affection's offering ;
Close the door from sight and sound
Of the busy world around ;
And in patient watch remain
Till my Lord appear again !

Thomas Whytehead (1815-1843), 1842.

31

7. 7. 7. 7.

TAKE my life, and let it be
Consecrated, Lord, to Thee !
Take my moments and my days,
Let them flow in ceaseless praise.

Take my hands, and let them move
At the impulse of Thy love ;
Take my feet, and let them be
Swift and beautiful for Thee.

Take my voice, and let me sing
Always, only, for my King ;
Take my lips, and let them be
Filled with messages from Thee.

Take my silver and my gold,
Not a mite would I withhold ;
Take my intellect, and use
Every power as Thou shalt choose.

Take my will, and make it Thine !
It shall be no longer mine ;
Take my heart, it is Thine own,
It shall be Thy royal throne.

Take my love ; my Lord, I pour
At Thy feet its treasured store :
Take myself, and I will be
Ever, only, all for Thee.

Frances Ridley Havergal (1836-1879), 1873.

ᵥ 32

TE lucis ante terminum,
Rerum Creator, poscimus,
Ut solita clementia
Sis praesul ad custodiam.

Procul recedant somnia,
Et noctium phantasmata,
Hostemque nostrum comprime,
Ne polluantur corpora.

Praesta, Pater omnipotens,
Per Iesum Christum Dominum,
Qui tecum in perpetuum
Regnat cum sancto Spiritu.

St. Ambrose, Bishop of Milan (340-397).

33

TE splendor et virtus Patris,
Te vita, Iesu, cordium,
Ab ore qui pendent tuo,
Laudamus inter Angelos.

Tibi mille densa millium
Ducum corona militat :
Sed explicat victor crucem
Michael salutis signifer.

Draconis hic dirum caput
In ima pellit tartara,
Ducemque cum rebellibus
Coelesti ab arce fulminat.

Contra ducem superbiae
Sequamur hunc nos Principem,
Ut detur ex Agni throno
Nobis corona gloriae.

Patri, simulque Filio,
Tibique, sancte Spiritus,
Sicut fuit, sit iugiter
Saeclum per omne gloria.

Hymn for St. Michael's Day (Roman Breviary) by
Rabanus Maurus, Abp. of Mentz (786-856).

34

TEACH me, my God and King,
  In all things Thee to see ;
And, what I do in anything,
  To do it as for Thee.

A man, that looks on glass,
  On it may stay his eye ;
Or, if he pleaseth, through it pass,
  And then the heav'n espy.

All may of Thee partake :
  Nothing can be so mean,
Which with this tincture, FOR THY SAKE,
  Will not grow bright and clean.

A servant with this clause
  Makes drudgery divine :
Who sweeps a room, as for Thy laws,
  Makes that, and th' action, fine.

This is the famous stone
  That turneth all to gold ;
For that, which God doth touch and own,
  Cannot for less be told.

George Herbert (1593-1632).

THOUGH lowly here our lot may be,
    High work have we to do,
In noble deeds to follow Him
    Whose lot was lowly too.

Our lives, enriched with gentle thoughts
    And loving deeds, may be
A stream that still the nobler grows
    The nearer to the sea.

To duty firm, to conscience true,
    However tried and pressed,
In God's clear sight high work we do,   .
    If we but do our best.

Thus we may make the lowliest lot
    With rays of glory bright ;
Thus we may turn a crown of thorns,
    Into a crown of light !

William Gaskell.

ᵥ 36

VENI, Creator Spiritus,
Mentes tuorum visita,
Imple superna gratia
Quae tu creasti pectora.

Qui Paraclitus diceris,
Deique donum altissimi,
Fons vivus, ignis, caritas,
Et spiritalis unctio :

Tu septiformis munere,
Dextrae Dei tu digitus,
Tu rite promisso Patris
Sermone ditans guttura :

Accende lumen sensibus,
Infunde amorem cordibus,
Infirma nostri corporis
Virtute firmans perpeti.

Hostem repellas longius,
Pacemque dones protinus,
Ductore sic te praevio
Vitemus omne noxium.

Per te sciamus da Patrem,
Noscamus atque Filium,
Et utriusque Spiritum
Credamus omni tempore.

Pope Gregory the Great (550-604).

37

WE may not climb the heavenly steeps
  To bring the Lord Christ down ;
In vain we search the lowest deeps,
  For Him no depths can drown.

But warm, sweet, tender, even yet
  A present help is He ;
And faith has yet its Olivet,
  And love its Galilee.

The healing of His seamless dress
  Is by our beds of pain ;
We touch Him in life's throng and press,
  And we are whole again.

Through Him the first fond prayers are said
  Our lips of childhood frame ;
The last low whispers of our dead
  Are burdened with His Name.

O Lord and Master of us all !
  Whate'er our name or sign :
We own Thy sway, we hear Thy call,
  We test our lives by Thine.

We faintly hear, we dimly see,
  In differing phrase we pray ;
But dim or clear, we own in Thee
  The Life, the Truth, the Way.

J. G. Whittier.

38

WE scatter seeds with careless hand,
And dream we ne'er shall see them more ;
    But for a thousand years
    Their fruit appears
    In weeds that mar the land,
    Or healthful store.

The deeds we do, the words we say,
Into still air they seem to fleet,
    We count them ever past,
    But they shall last :
    In the long future they
    And we shall meet.

                    John Keble (1792-1866).

39

WE walk on earth, and to its ways
  Our time and thoughts are given,
Yet, amid all its busiest days,
  Our hearts may be in heaven.

Nothing so lightens the dull load
  Life's urgent claims impose,
As close communion with our God :
  It is our best repose.

When vexed with ills which we despair
  To bafile or control,
The lifting of the heart in prayer
  Sheds sunshine on the soul.

When disappointed in the love
  We leaned on too secure,
What joy it is to look above,
  And feel one Friend is sure !

When, wearied with life's ebb and flow,
  We for still waters sigh ;
O how it sweetens change below
  To think of rest on high !

Thus we in peace our souls possess,
  Though all around be fear,
Full of the blessèd consciousness
  That heaven is sure and near.

Dark clouds may o'er us threatening stand,
  We can sing on, and smile ;
The sunshine of the cloudless land
  Lies round us all the while.

We can bear any cross or grief,
  If, with their gloom, be given
This one sweet secret of relief,
  To keep our thoughts in heaven.

                  J. S. B. Monsell (1811-1875).

40

WHAT conscience dictates to be done,
  Or warns me not to do,
This, teach me more than hell to shun,
  That, more than heaven pursue.

If I am right, Thy grace impart
  Still in the right to stay ;
If I am wrong, O teach my heart
  To find that better way.

Save me alike from foolish pride,
  Or impious discontent,
At aught Thy wisdom has denied,
  Or aught Thy goodness lent.

Teach me to feel another's woe,
  To hide the fault I see ;
The mercy I to others show,
  That mercy show to me.

       Alexander Pope (1688-1744).

WHEN quiet in my house I sit,
　Thy book is my companion still ;
My joy Thy sayings to repeat,
　Talk o'er the records of Thy will,
And search the oracles divine,
Till every heart-felt word be mine.

O may the gracious words divine
　Subject of all my converse be :
So will the Lord His follower join,
　And walk and talk Himself with me ;
So shall my heart His presence prove,
And burn with everlasting love.

Oft as I lay me down to rest,
　O may the reconciling word
Sweetly compose my weary breast !
　While, on the bosom of my Lord,
I sink in blissful dreams away,
And visions of eternal day.

Rising to sing my Saviour's praise,
　Thee may I publish all day long ;
And let Thy precious word of grace
　Flow from my heart, and fill my tongue ;
Fill all my life with purest love,
And join me to the church above !

　　　　　Charles Wesley (1708-1788), 1762.

INDICES.

INDEX OF SUBJECTS.

INDEX OF AUTHORS.

INDEX OF FIRST LINES.

—

E E 2

THE END.